SCRAP CRAFT

Ideas for Holidays and Parties

SCRAP CRAFT

Ideas for Holidays and Parties

by Elizabeth D. Logan

with diagrams by June K. Ciancio

CHARLES SCRIBNER'S SONS · NEW YORK

COLOR PRINTED IN JAPAN

TEXT AND BLACK AND WHITE ILLUSTRATIONS
PRINTED IN THE UNITED STATES OF AMERICA
Library of Congress Catalog Card Number   72-7730
SBN 684-13206-0

For Pete's memory

ACKNOWLEDGMENTS

My deepest thanks to my numerous friends and relations who over the years have tirelessly collected mounds of scrap materials for me, not only items that I have requested, but new and obscure materials of which I was unaware. . . .

. . . to Ellen Yard of Wm. E. Wright Co. and to Ruth Moore for help with special materials . . .

. . . to photographers Richard Bianchi, Mike Bonvino, Srdjan Maljkovic, Howard Malofsky, Gil O'Conner, and especially Bruce Elkus for my education in their medium . . .

. . . to Anita Wiener, Stuart R. Mc Leod, and George A. Ouellette, Jr. for their suggestions and encouragement with the manuscript . . .

. . . to Elinor Parker, my editor, and Margareta F. Lyons, my book designer.

CONTENTS

PREFACE

Scrap craft is the art of making something new from refuse—discarded or found materials. Recycling is the current popular term for this. Scrap craft can be made wholly or in part from refuse, more frequently from a combination of new and old materials. They are often used out of context (used in ways for which they were not originally intended), as substitutes for more costly or harder to find supplies.

All our material culture originated in this way. The first man who gnawed the meat from a bone and tossed it away, only to retrieve it later to use as a tool or to fashion one from it, was one of the two originators of this process, our craft. The other was the man who picked up a rock or stick and used it also as a tool or weapon. Perhaps this latter honor really belongs to a creature lower on the evolutionary scale, such as the sea otter who dives for rocks, then floating on his back, lays them on his stomach and pounds mollusks open against them.

As early as the Upper Paleolithic, man has made a pretty good collection of scrap crafts for himself: stone, bone and wooden weapons and tools; flint points; bone needles; ivory and horn implements; skin clothing; pigments and brushes for wall paintings; skin vessels; and stone lamps. All of these, in fact all of his manufactured possessions, were made from materials that he had either found or had originally discarded and later learned to collect or save for future use.

Our ancestors on the American frontier carried on this prehistoric tradition and lived by the philosophy of "waste not want not," "use it up, wear it out, make it do, do without." They made their own fabrics, from yarn they had spun themselves. When bedding and clothing wore out, the still solid parts of the textiles were made into curtains, smaller garments, bags, etc. When these in turn wore out, the remnants went into the scrap bag to be used again for patchwork quilts and rag rugs.

Although we are now a nation of predominantly urban and suburban dwellers, many can still recall their rural childhoods when nothing was allowed to go to waste. "A farmer saves everything" was close to literally true. And that everything was often repaired with bailing wire and used for a new or different job.

In our urban industrial society we are only beginning to realize first that we still live on found objects, for industry exists on raw materials (read: found materials); and second that we had better do something quickly about the discarded materials that are polluting our environment. It has been said that "the amount of refuse produced by a materialistic society is the true index of its success." We are successful to the tune of five pounds of *household* waste *per person* per day in the United States.

In other words, we are learning that we must come full circle to that prehistoric, pioneer, and rural philosophy of reutilizing materials, if we are not to destroy our way of life, our environment, and ourselves. Each of us pollutes to a greater or less degree, but each is guilty and has a responsibility to change this pattern of conspicuous waste.

Scrap crafts will not solve this problem, but they will make us more aware of its extent. As we learn to look at discards with an eye for new uses, we become aware of what a colossal amount of useful junk goes into our trash cans each day. Plastic alone, that cheap and indestructible product, can be salvaged for dozens of uses.

Of that five pounds per person per day of household trash, 70 per cent is in packaging in one form or another—50 per cent paper, 7 per cent glass, 7 per cent metal, and 5 per cent (but growing fast) plastic. Therefore, look at each container and wrapper for a possible craft use before you discard it. Study the projects in this book and play a game with yourself and your family: think of new uses for the discards that are used here, both in the projects and in the lists of scrap on pages 14–19, and think of other discards that can be substituted for these. Make collections of various packages and containers in large corrugated boxes, marking each large box for a particular category such as plastics, aluminum cans, bottles and jars, bottle tops, waxed cardboard containers, etc.

Learn to open wrapping papers so that they are not torn, to smooth, fold and store them for future use.

All of this, of course, can only heighten the pleasure that is derived from scrap crafts. To the joy of accomplishment that all crafts bring is added the fillip that the object has cost less both economically and environmentally.

Always remember that according to Sir Walter Scott no less a person than King Charles II reported, "As my canny subjects in Scotland say, 'If you keep a thing seven years, you are sure to find a use for it at last.'" Let us add that if you are clever and determined, you'll find a use for it long before the seven years.

SCRAP CRAFT

Ideas for Holidays and Parties

How to Use
This Book

BE SURE TO READ THIS SECTION FIRST, BEFORE BEGINNING WORK

Although this book deals with projects for parties and holidays, it offers a wide enough sampling to give you a perspective of the almost limitless possibilities of the crafts. After making these projects and learning the procedures and techniques they involve, you will be ready to branch out in any direction that takes your fancy. The suggestions given for work spaces, equipment, supplies, and collection of scrap materials are comprehensive enough for more advanced work.

Each project is self-contained so that you can begin with any one that you wish, regardless of its position in the book.

In *General Directions* there is a collection of basic techniques that are applicable to a number of projects or that will be useful as a reference in improvising new designs and in using other scrap materials. The directions for each project are complete except for references to these special techniques which are referred to by page number.

The majority of patterns are given full size and can simply be traced from the page or pages, but be *sure* to read the directions first for tracing on page 22, item 9 before you begin. When patterns are too large to be reproduced full size, they can be enlarged on 1-inch graph paper by following the directions on page 24, item 12.

Measurements are sometimes specified, sometimes omitted, depending on the nature of the object. Where they are omitted, the size is either obvious from the materials and photograph or is unimportant.

Many of the ideas incorporated in these projects can be used in numerous variations: figures can be made on a variety of bases with many different materials; party bouquets such as the flower hearts from the Valentine party can be adapted to other themes; and Christmas ornaments can be made from almost any small pieces of scrap.

It is wise not to strain too hard to be neat. If you have a natural proclivity for it, by all means proceed accordingly, but don't feel that it is necessary. Many clumsy, even sloppy individuals have extraordinary creative gifts. It is a sorry comment on our national obsession with neatness and cleanliness (despite the way we litter our environment) that so often these gifts are allowed to atrophy because they cannot be expressed within our convention of tight, mechanical exactitude. It is better if these gifted individuals sail in and work, letting the ragged edges remain uneven and globs of paint and glue fall where they will. The results will have a freedom, freshness, and verve that too often are lacking from overprecise work. As an incentive to freshness, the patterns have been drawn loosely and without perfect symmetry. Despite this, hints are included in a number of projects on how to keep your work tidy and unsmeared for those who want to know.

It is best to remember, however, that spontaneity of execution and strength of design are the two important qualities in any creative craft.

Work Area, Storage, Tools, Equipment, and Supplies

Below are suggestions for work areas, equipment, tools, and supplies. These are for (1) a beginner, (2) an individual with a steady hobby, and (3) a full-time worker. The first and second work for individual satisfaction and pleasure. The third may also work for pleasure—as a dedicated hobbyist with the leisure to make gifts for family and friends and contributions for charity sales and bazaars. She may, however, be engaged in a small home business.

WORK AREA

A table at a convenient height, a good light, and a comfortable straight chair are your basic requirements. Add to these 2 or 3 large sheets, 23 x 40 inches, of heavy cardboard (not corrugated) to protect the table top and to give you a good work surface. Cutting, punching, and painting can be done on them without damaging the table.

If you are short of space, the dining room or kitchen table will answer the first of these requirements. Since materials and equipment must be removed between work periods, try to find storage space close at hand to avoid wasting time and energy each time you set up your work area.

A better solution, if you have more space, is to set aside a special table in a corner of a room for a permanent "studio." A screen can hide it when it is not in use. Unfinished work can be left on the table and covered with a sheet of clear plastic or with a plastic bag from the cleaners to protect it from dust. Cabinets, shelves, and/or a chest of drawers can be arranged along the walls to hold materials and equipment.

LIGHT

If possible, use a 300-watt overhead fixture, supplemented by a Tensor work light on the table. If more than one person is working at the table you will need 2 or more lamps on it.

STORAGE

A collection of cardboard boxes to stack in the corner will suffice until you begin to get a good collection of scrap and supplies. Later, plastic boxes of various sizes from tiny to large, a wide chest with narrow drawers to hold papers, a few card index files for small objects, the cardboard boxes, and a bookshelf (with doors or a curtain to keep out dust) to hold the boxes and miscellaneous materials will give you ample storage space. You can find most of these in stores for second-hand office furniture and in junk shops.

CLOTHESLINE

When making Christmas ornaments or other hanging items, a thin clothesline strung across the corner of the room will be useful. Use spring clothespins and large safety pins to hang up the finished objects.

MATERIALS AND TOOLS

Below is a suggested assortment of equipment, tools and supplies that you will need. You will not have to have all of these immediately, so don't be alarmed by the number. (If you are short of funds or appalled at the prospect of acquiring so many pieces of equipment to make just a few objects of scrap, take heart.) Read over the instructions for your first project and check them for the tools and supplies that will be required. Assemble these, complete the project and then go on to your second one. This time you will already have a number of the things required and when you have gotten the extra ones for this project you will be in fairly good shape for your third project.

At first buy only as many tools as are absolutely necessary. If you find with experience that you are spending time and deriving pleasure, perhaps even profit, from your hobby, then gradually add to your collection. There is no pleasure quite like that of splurging on a useful, long-desired, and really good piece of equipment. But do not overdo it. Many a beginner has swamped herself with purchases; and in the pleasure of acquiring them, has failed to give preference to those that are basic. In their place she has collected specialized gadgets that are seldom needed. Give yourself time to learn what you really need to build up a useful and pleasant work shop. The same admonitions are equally applicable to the purchase of supplies: proceed with caution and acquire slowly.

Your most used tools, equipment, and supplies should be kept on your work table. Begin with:

pencils	ruler
scissors	stapler
Scotch tape	Sobo and Uhu glues
rubber cement	pins
thumb tacks	push pins
paper clips	gluing glass (see p. 28, item 23)

You will soon need:

small-parts cabinet

One measuring $9\frac{1}{2}$ inches high, 10 inches wide, and 6 inches deep with clear plastic drawers takes up little space on the table and helps keep your work area free of clutter. At first it will hold the small items from the above list. Gradually add:

erasers	pen knife
single-edged razor blades	spools of fine wire
compass	spool of nylon fishing line
tweezers	nylon transparent thread
rubber bands	

Dental tweezers are particularly useful. Collect several kinds and sizes of tweezers. On top of the cabinet keep:

staple remover

Find a place on the table for tape dispensers for the following tapes:

Scotch	magic mending
double-stick	masking

Near the center of the table place:

plastic kitchen lazy susan

and on it jars to hold:

pencils	pens
colored pencils	felt-tipped marking pens
brushes	bamboo and metal skewers

It will also hold:

jar of rubber cement	Sobo glue
can of cement thinner	small bottle of gold paint
small cup of tooth picks	additional items you may find
India ink	useful

The table should also accommodate:

draftsman's triangle	large paper shears
paperweight	spring clothespins
pad of tracing paper	plastic French curve

The family tool chest will supply your basic tools:

saw	hammer
pliers	pincers
screwdriver	

Later add:

long-nose pliers	jig-saw
awl	brace and bit
C clamps of various sizes	wire cutters

If the family boasts a few power tools, they will be invaluable, particularly:

electric jig saw	drill

At the hardware store buy:

nails   nuts and bolts
tacks   steel washers
screws

all in a variety of sizes. Store these in small screw-top jars, such as those for baby food, on shelves by your work table. Also keep on these shelves:

jars of poster paint   spray paint
acrylic paints   water colors
small and large plastic boxes to   sandpaper of various grades
   hold fragile scrap   pipe cleaners
paint rags   green-enameled florist's wire

The medicine chest will yield:

cotton balls   Q-tip swabs
medicine dropper   cuticle scissors

Your sewing basket and cabinet will supply:

needles   thread
thimbles   corsage pins
tape measure   glass-headed pins
snaps, hooks and eyes   common pins
dressmaker's carbon papers in   sequin pins
   various colors   safety pins
embroidery, pinking, and scallop   dressmaker's ruler and marking
   shears   guide

It is wise not to use sewing scissors except for fabrics, as paper soon dulls them. Mark fabric shears with small triangles of red plastic tape beside the screw on both sides. Buy other scissors for paper and leave them unmarked so that you can tell the two apart. Collect a variety of sizes and kinds for both uses. The manufacturers of pinking and scallop shears recommend their use for both paper and fabric. If you can afford it, it is safer to have separate pairs for each material.
From your household closet use:

steam iron   sleeve board
ironing board   pressing mitt
pressing cloth   tailor's cushion

From your kitchen:

ice pick	bowls
jars	shelf paper
glasses for water, etc.	sponges
soap	dish cloths
soap powder	food coloring
liquid dishwashing detergent	

Adhesives, Fumes, and Tapes

ADHESIVES

Sobo glue, Uhu glue, silicone adhesive, and rubber cement are recommended for use.

Other white glues can be substituted for Sobo, but their consistency is not as satisfactory. If you are doing a large amount of gluing with Sobo, keep a damp cloth, a small flat-bottomed bowl of water, and a hand towel beside you on the table. As soon as your hands become sticky, clean and dry them. It makes the job easier and quicker. If a drop of Sobo falls on a piece of fabric, allow it to stand untouched until it is dry. It can then be picked off with the fingers.

The advantages of Uhu glue are: It dries quickly and has many of the properties of household cements. Unlike them it does not dissolve Styrofoam and plastics if used in moderate amounts. It will hold on smooth plastic surfaces. It can be removed *immediately* after application, but *not* later, by rubbing and rolling into small balls.

Silicone adhesive holds materials such as stone, glass, and ceramics. If possible, use the clear variety because it is less likely to show.

Rubber cement is ideal for temporary jobs with paper and cardboard, but it is not permanent over a period of years. It can eventually rot paper, as well as stain some kinds. Bear this in mind when you are making items that are expected to last indefinitely. Excess rubber cement can be removed by rubbing and rolling into a ball. If the cement has dried and you wish to remove it from a surface, coat the area with fresh cement and let it stand briefly. It will usually come up when rubbed. If it has stained the paper when it has just been put on, coat the entire paper and rub it off. Usually the stain will disappear.

FUMES

Silicone adhesive; acetone; epoxy; and spray cans of paint, adhesive, fixative, and Krylon should be used *only* in a well-ventilated room with a large exhaust fan in an open window. As many people have a poor tolerance for the fumes of felt-tipped marking pens it is wise to use them only for brief periods or in a room with the fan in the open window. The fumes from Uhu glue and rubber cement can be unpleasant if inhaled for any length of time. Turpentine in a closed room will give some people headaches. It is better to be overcautious than to take chances with fumes from any new or unfamiliar product. Even more caution is needed with flammable materials, particularly rubber cement thinner. Beware of using it if there is an open flame in the vicinity, even in an adjoining room. This includes the pilot light of the kitchen stove. Do *not* smoke around an open container of thinner.

Study the labels on all volatile materials and proceed with caution.

TAPES

Scotch and double-stick tapes are fine for temporary jobs, but eventually their adhesive becomes sticky, loosens, and stains the surface to which it was attached.

Magic mending tape is long-lasting, but more expensive than Scotch.

Masking tape is fine for sealing boxes to keep out dust. It is longer-lasting than Scotch, but is not as permanent as magic mending.

Filament tape, though designed primarily for mailing, is extremely strong and is excellent for binding heavy objects and materials together.

Use package tape for sealing boxes to keep out dust as well as for mailing.

How to Collect Scrap

Sort, store, and label scrap materials as you acquire them; it will save endless frustration later.

WHERE TO FIND IT

Aside from your household discards, you should acquire scrap by collecting from anyone and everyone. Ask friends to be on the lookout for it. They may have access to particular or unusual materials on their jobs. Friends working in offices, laboratories, garages, factories, hospitals, restaurants, and stores will all find different kinds of scrap to salvage for you. Be sure that they know you want it and that you will appreciate their thoughtfulness in saving it for you.

Ask the men you know to save their neckties and cummerbunds. Ask the women to save dressmaking and sewing scraps. Haunt second-hand, thrift, and junk stores, particularly the last. Become friendly with the proprietors and they will often take a real interest in turning up "bargains in junk" for you.

If you are involved in work for a club, charity, church, or youth organization, you can collect large supplies of usable refuse by contacting executives, managers and proprietors of local

bakeries	carpenter shops
binderies	department stores
box manufacturers	fabric houses
builders' supply firms	factories
cabinetmakers	florist shops
candy stores	florist supply houses

hardware stores

lumber yards

packaging manufacturers

paint stores

paper companies

photography studios

printing houses

newspapers

restaurants

restaurant supply houses

rug stores

supermarkets

LISTS OF MATERIALS

Below are partial lists of scrap that can be used for crafts. They are only a beginning. You will find countless other items to add to your supply.

WOOD SCRAPS

HOUSEHOLD

beads

broomsticks

children's blocks

cigar boxes

clip clothespins

curtain rings

excelsior

fireplace matches

florist sticks

flower stakes

ice cream sticks

lollipop and popsicle sticks

match sticks

orange sticks

pencil stubs

salad forks and spoons

sawdust and pencil shavings

small wooden boxes

tongue depressors

wooden spools

wooden spoons

LUMBER-YARD SCRAPS

balls

dowels

finials and turned pieces

laths

moldings

scraps of:

board

hardboard

plywood

punchboard

PAPER AND CARDBOARD

PAPER

blotters

brown wrapping paper

butcher's paper

Christmas, Valentine cards

confetti
crepe paper (flameproof)
facial tissue
gift wrapping paper
lace-paper doilies
magazines
napkins and towels
newspapers

paper bags
paper baking cups
paper straws
tissue paper
typing paper
velour paper
Victorian "scrap"
wallpaper samples

CARDBOARD

apple-box dividers
boxes:
  large:
    corrugated
    gift
    hat
    shoe
    suit
  round:
    oatmeal
    salt
    spices
  small:
    cosmetic
    gift
    match
    pencil

boxes:
  small (continued)
    pill
    candy
cartons:
  cheese
  egg
  ice cream
  milk
  sour cream
tubes:
  towel cores
  mailing tubes
corrugated board
corrugated paper
other containers:
  bouillon cube tubes

PLASTIC

acetate
bags:
  cleaners' for clothes
  food
  garbage
  storage
baskets for berries
  and tomatoes
cellophane
celluloid

cellulose sponges
Con-Tact scraps
cosmetic containers:
  cold cream jars
  compacts
  lipstick cases
  powder boxes
  rouge containers
curlers and pins
dishes

egg cartons
freezer dishes
lace doilies
opaque bleach bottles
opaque liquid dye bottles
packing:
    bubbled wrapping
    molded forms
    pellets
pill bottles and boxes

polyethylene chemist tubing
refrigerator dishes
sheets and pads of foam
spools from electric typewriters
styrofoam forms, trays, etc.
table cloths
tops for bottles and jars
transparent bottles
tumblers

FABRIC, CLOTHING, DRESSMAKER'S FINDINGS, FIBERS

FABRICS

beamus bagging
buckram
burlap
canvas
carpet samples
cotton batting

dress fabric scraps
jersey curls
lamb's wool
monk's cloth
oil cloth
upholstery samples

CLOTHING

dresses
fabric gloves
felt:
    belts
    handbags
    hats
    jackets
    pennants
    skirts
fur:
    coats
    collars
    hats
    muffs
    rugs
    scraps
garters
girdles

discarded jewelry
leather:
    belts
    gloves
    handbags
    hats
    jackets
    purses
    robes
mittens
neckties
scarves
shirts
shoe laces
socks
stockings and panty hose
sweaters
underwear

DRESSMAKER'S FINDINGS

balled curtain fringe	laces
beads	novelty trims
braids	ribbons
buttons	rickrack
dress frogs	ruching
feathers	ruffling
fringes	sequins

HOUSEHOLD SCRAPS

terry cloth:	curtains
bath mats	sheets
towels	table cloths
wash cloths	

FIBERS

clotheslines	string
cords	thread
embroidery floss	twine
rope	yarn

METALS

ballpoint pens	eyelets for shoes
bobby pins	expanded metal
brass-headed nails	grommets
brass paper fasteners	hairpins
brads	hooks:
buckles:	clothes
belt	picture
shoe	shower curtain
cans:	keys
candy	light sockets and parts
spices	lipstick cases
tobacco	locks
chains	mascara tubes and brushes
clock parts	metal scraps (plain and rusted)
coathangers	pins:
corroded metal with patina	tidy

florist   bottle
Polaroid camera cartridges   jar
potato skewers   tube
pull tabs   wire:
radio parts   bailing
roof tins   barbed
screening   chicken
screweyes   florist:
sheet metal   flexible
shoe taps   rigid
sleigh bells   wrapped
spools from cameras   mesh
steel wool   soldering wire
tops:

MISCELLANEOUS

FOOD

bones: cereals and pasta
    animal   cake decorations:
    fish   silver balls
    poultry   dragees
candies: icing
    hard   colored sugars
    wrapped   colored balls
ice cream cones   sugar cubes
lobster claws

NATURAL PRODUCTS (VEGETABLE)

bark   mosses
branches   nuts
cornhusks   nut shells
dried flowers   pine cones and needles
driftwood   reeds
ferns   seeds
fruit   straw
gourds   twigs
grasses   vegetables
leaves   weeds

NATURAL PRODUCTS (MINERAL AND ANIMAL)

flat pebbles

marble

rough stones

sand

shells

GLASS

bottles

flitter

flashbulbs

iridescent balls

jars

lightbulbs (all kinds and sizes)

marbles

mirrors

tumblers

HOUSEHOLD AND GARAGE

auto tires

balloons

BB shots

broom straws

candles

corks

lamp shades

linoleum

modeling clay

picture frames

plaster of paris

sealing wax

tiles

General Directions

Following is a collection of basic techniques that are applicable to a number of projects or that will be useful as a reference in improvising new designs and using other scrap materials. For additional reference material, become familiar with the project instructions. These give other techniques not listed here.

CLEAN AND STORE SCRAP

Cans   Containers: wash and dry metal cans, bottles and food containers.

1. Save some steel cans intact. If space is scarce, remove the tops and bottoms of others, cut open the sides along the seam, and nest the curved metal rectangles inside one another for storage.

For aluminum cans, cut through the rim at spout or opening A in diagram and cut away the top just along the ridge or shoulder, B in diagram 1. Once you have started cutting, you can pull up the top with a pair of pliers, diagram 2. Carefully pull it off. If possible, it is wise to

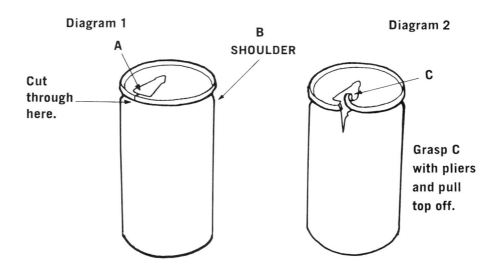

Diagram 1

A

B
SHOULDER

Cut
through
here.

Diagram 2

C

Grasp C
with pliers
and pull
top off.

enlist a man's help for this. Once the top has been removed, the going is comparatively easy. Cut down the side of the can to the bottom, then around the bottom to remove it. This can be done with scissors. Flatten out the rectangle of aluminum and save the bottom, too.

2. Open packages without tearing paper. Smooth paper flat, fold and store in box or on shelf.

Wrapping paper

3. Always open gift packages very carefully, using a knife to cut the tape that holds down the overlap and the flaps on the ends. Then remove bows that are attached with double-stick tape, by pulling the bow from the tape and leaving it attached to the paper. Remove tape and adhesive with rubber-cement thinner; or place a piece of paper over the tape and run a warm iron over it. Remove any remaining adhesive with thinner.

Gift-wrapping paper

Press entire piece of wrapping paper with a warm iron. If it is crumpled or has folds in the wrong places, crumple the entire sheet; then iron it flat. If crumpled uniformly, it will look as though the creases were intentional and were part of the original design. It will also give the paper an interesting texture and can even make a poorly designed paper look more attractive.

Store in large shallow drawers or wrap around a cardboard mailing tube. Cover with tissue paper or plastic cleaner's bag to protect from dust.

4. Press ribbon with warm iron and wrap around large tape cores or a fat mailing tube. Cover with a plastic cleaner's bag to protect from dust, if stored on open shelf.

Ribbons

5. Store loosely in plastic bags. Tie the neck of the bags to keep out dust. Store where nothing heavy can fall or be placed on them.

Bows and pompons

6. Remove candy carefully from cup. Soak cup in hot, soapy water, rinse, and drain dry. Crease folds of fluting between fingers. Store in plastic boxes.

Chocolate foil cups

To use the foil flat: open cup out, soak in soapy water, rinse, and drain dry. Press foil on flat surface. Use fingertip and then fingernail to smooth. Stack and store in small plastic box.

7. Use rubber-cement thinner to clean, with a soft piece of cloth or a cotton ball. Store in plastic box.

Plastic spool from electric typewriter

Neckties   8. Use embroidery scissors to snip stitches down underside of tie and open seam. Remove center lining or linings and separate. Open hems at ends of tie. If ends are lined, turn inside out and carefully open seams. Press all parts with a steam iron.

Ties make excellent clothes for small figures. Generally the patterns are small and the fabric soft enough to fit the scale of even 3-inch figures.

Tracing, pocket   9. It is very important when tracing patterns from the book that you *always* first cover the page or pages with a sheet or sheets of heavy acetate, clear or frosted. Make a pocket to hold two sheets of it and glue the pocket to the inside back cover of the book. Use the sheets and always replace them before closing the book, so that they will not get lost.

Pocket: See diagram. Cut 2 sheets of acetate the size of the book's pages. Lay one on a piece of tag board and trace around it. Remove. Divide the rectangle on the board diagonally from the upper-right-hand corner to the lower-left-hand corner. Draw a half-inch margin around the bottom and right-hand side. Cut out the lower triangle with the margins intact. Score along the dotted lines.

Spread glue along the margins and fold them under. Place the pocket inside the back cover of the book, flush with the bottom and right-hand edges, press down and allow to dry. If necessary, trim the edges of the two sheets of acetate so that they can be slipped easily into the pocket.

If you neglect to use the acetate, your pencil will scar and eventually wear through the paper. Many a pattern book has slowly but surely been destroyed in this way.

When you have the acetate in place, lay a sheet of tracing paper over it and trace your design onto the paper.

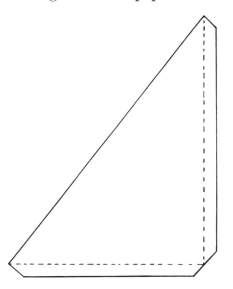

To transfer the design to the material of your project, use a piece of carbon paper, either typewriter or dressmakers'. If these are not available, turn the tracing paper over. With a very soft, thick pencil, go over the lines on the back. Reverse the paper again, tape it onto the material, and draw over the original lines with enough pressure to transfer the soft pencil on the back onto the material.

On certain surfaces, such as burlap or felt, this process will not work. Instead, use a heavy darning needle to punch holes at intervals along the lines. Be sure that the holes are clean and open. Pin or tape the tracing paper to the material. Use a white or colored pencil to make dots on it through the holes. When complete, remove the tracing paper and with the same pencil join the dots to make continuous lines.

10. Extend line AC to the desired height, line EC.
    Draw horizontal at right angles to it, EH.
    Draw diagonal through points C and B and extend until line intercepts EH at F.
    Drop a perpendicular (at right angle to EH) at point F to form line FJ.
    Extend line CD until it intercepts FJ at point G.
    The rectangle CEFG has the same proportions as ABCD
Reverse process to reduce.

To enlarge or reduce a rectangle

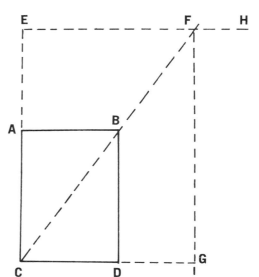

11. To draw straight line A parallel to a second line, B, measure the required distance C at 3 points. Mark each point with a dot. Use a ruler to draw a line through these dots.

Parallel lines

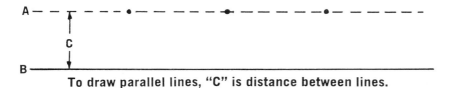

To draw parallel lines, "C" is distance between lines.

To enlarge by
squares

12. Most of the designs to be enlarged in the book were originally drawn on a 1-inch grid and then reduced. To enlarge, simply use 1-inch graph paper or draw a grid of 1-inch squares on shelf or brown paper. In each square of the enlargement, draw the same lines to scale that appear in the corresponding square on the pattern (see diagrams below). To make work easier, number corresponding squares.

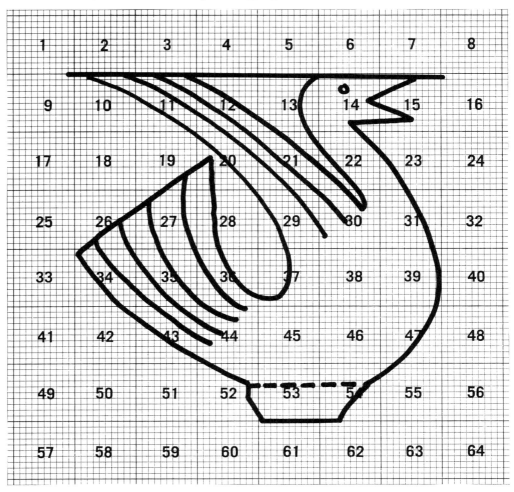

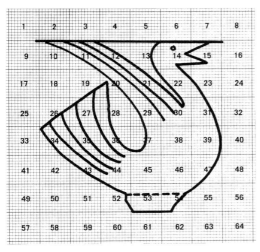

13. Diagram 1. With A as center, draw arc CD with radius of more than half the distance of AB.
    Using same radius, draw EF with point B as center.
    Where arcs intercept at points H and G, draw a line connecting them.
    Center of line AB is where it intercepts GH at J.
    Line GH is perpendicular and at right angles to AB.
    Angles AJG, GJB, etc., are right angles.
Or use a draftsman's triangle to do any of these.

To draw a perpendicular and a right angle and to divide a line in half

14. Diagram 2. Using point A as center, draw a circle.
    Draw line through A, intercepting circle through B and C.
    With B and C as centers, set up perpendicular to BC at A, intercepting circle at D and E.
    Repeat process at points B, C, D, and E to divide into $\frac{1}{8}$'s at F and G.

To divide a circle into $\frac{1}{2}$'s, $\frac{1}{4}$'s, and $\frac{1}{8}$'s

15. Draw a circle and using the radius, divide the circumference into arcs. These will be approximately even, and for practical purposes can be used as $\frac{1}{6}$'s.

To divide a circle into $\frac{1}{6}$'s

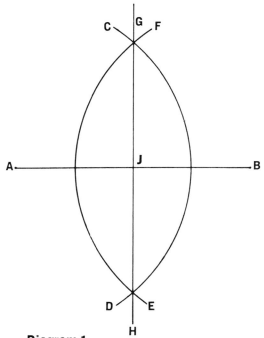

Diagram 1

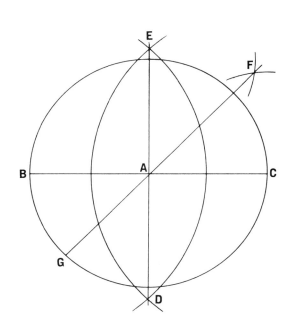

Diagram 2

5-pointed star

16. Draw a circle with diameter BC.
Erect perpendicular AD at center A.
Divide AC in half to find point E.
With center E use radius ED to find point F.
With center D use radius DF to find point G.
Radius DG = ⅕ of circumference.

Divide circumference in ⅕'s. Draw lines GK, GJ, DH, DJ, and HK to make 5-pointed star.

These stars can also be traced, enlarged and reduced by drawing lines parallel to their outlines.

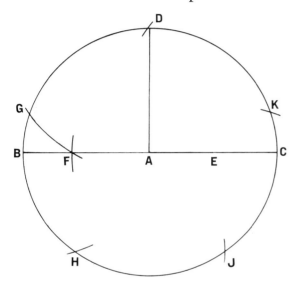
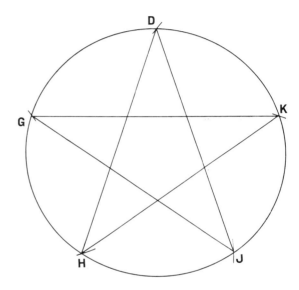

3-dimensional 5-pointed star

17. Draw a 5-pointed star in a circle following directions above. Cut out circle. Draw inner circle as in diagram and cut along dotted lines to *edge* of inner circle. Fold along center lines of star points to form ridges in center; fold center line of each V in to form valley. Crease along edges of star and fold flaps under. Trim flaps along edges of points into triangles

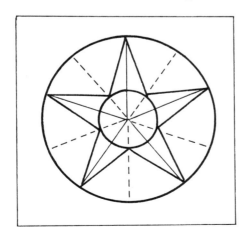
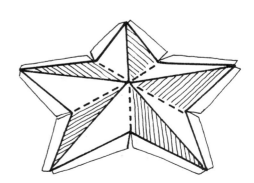

that can be overlapped and joined on underside with masking tape. This will make star 3-dimensional and also form pockets behind the star's points. Cut triangles of cardboard and glue them into these pockets.

18. Cut out a semicircle. Pinch at center for tip, overlap straight sides, and roll to form cone. Secure overlap with staples, glue or tape.

Cone or conical roof

CONICAL ROOF

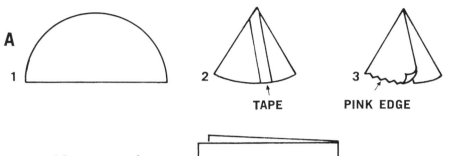

19. Fold a piece of paper lengthwise. Draw half of pattern on fold. Cut out, open, and spread flat.

Bi-symmetrical pattern

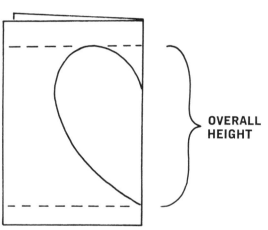

20. This can also be a snowflake or sunburst. Fold a square of paper diagonally in half, then into quarters by folding the triangle into halves. On this triangle fold both sides over one another to form thirds, as in step 3 of diagram. Cut ends into V and notch sides with scissors and paper punch. Open and spread flat.

Symmetrical lace-paper medallion

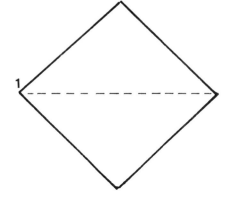
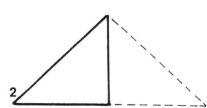
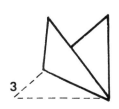
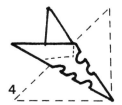

Multifold
paper cut-out

21. Accordion-pleat a strip of paper. Notch sides on folds and ends with scissors. Be careful not to join cuts from opposite sides. Open and spread flat.

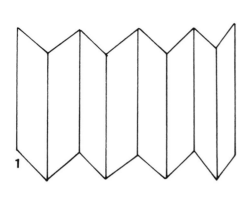  

BASIC PROCEDURES

To score and fold
paper, bristol board

22. Score lines with the blunt edge of a scissors' blade on paper and the sharp edge on bristol board. Fold along scored lines.

Gluing glass

23. Always use a glass for gluing. Use plastic tape to cover the edges of a sheet of glass 9 x 11 inches. Two glasses this size will be more useful than 1 large one.

Squeeze a small puddle of Sobo or Uhu glue in a corner of the glass, not on the tape. Use tweezers to dip the article to be glued into the puddle or use a toothpick to transfer glue from puddle onto object. Lay a long, narrow article on the glass; use the spout of the tube or bottle to run a line of glue down the article. Spread glue with a toothpick.

To clean glass, remove Uhu with a safety razor blade. Some areas of Sobo can be removed in the same way. For stubborn spots of Sobo, lay glass on drainboard of kitchen sink and spread a wet cloth over glass until glue is soft enough to be washed off.

To dry mount
or bond

24. Mix thoroughly 2 parts rubber cement with 1 part thinner. Coat 1 side of each piece of paper with this mixture. With a small piece of cardboard, such as a match-book cover, spread evenly and scrape off excess.

Lay a piece of tracing paper over the first sheet. Be sure that sheet is completely covered except for 1-inch border at one end. Lay second sheet of paper on top of tracing paper and align with first sheet. Press and smooth second sheet to first along 1-inch border until they adhere firmly. Gradually pull tracing paper out from under second a little at a time, smoothing and pressing it flat with a cloth. Be sure there are no wrinkles or bubbles each time before you pull out the tracing paper a few inches more. When tracing paper has been removed, rub entire surface of second sheet with cloth.

25. Adapt width and height of triangle to the shape of the panel or figure it will support. Cut out triangle and cut off upper tip. Score line CB. Trim bottom of line AB. This will keep figure or panel from tipping forward. Glue or staple flap D to back of figure or panel.

Easel to stand figures and objects upright

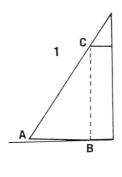
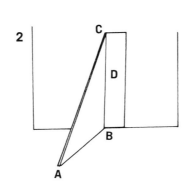

26. Paint Styrofoam with 3 coats of Sobo glue. Allow to dry between coats and be sure surface is completely covered. Apply acrylic paint over surface when last coat of glue is dry.

Acrylic paint on Styrofoam

27. Cut rectangle of cardboard and wrap with yarn or thread, once for a thin tassel, 3 or more times for a thick tassel or pompon. Tie strands together at top with thread. Cut strands across bottom to make ends free.

Tassel and pompon

For pompon, fluff and trim ends until short enough to form ball. Hold in vapor over steam from tea kettle to fluff ends of yarn or thread.

For tassel, wrap with yarn or thread to form "knot" at top (see drawing).

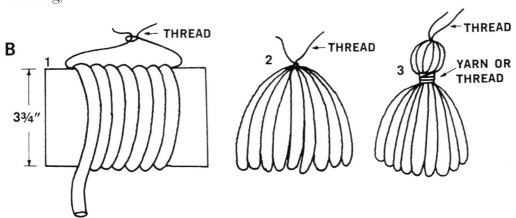

*Hair and beards
in various styles
and materials*

28. *Top row, opposite*

To shred metallic ribbon: cut off both lengthwise edges of ribbon, leaving ½-inch solid area at one end. Use a pin to pull out cross threads.

Joseph's beard: Cut 10 6-inch-long strips. Trim edges and unravel, leaving ½ inch intact at one end. Glue to face.

Hair: Cut 27 4-inch-long strips. Trim edges and unravel except for ½ inch at center. Use a scissors' blade to curl 18 of these strips. Leave top of head bare; glue strips around head in 2 layers. Glue remaining 9 uncurled in third layer beneath the first. Fluff ends.

Moustache: Twist together in the center the 2 remaining strips and glue to face.

Mary's hair: Cut 12 16-inch-long strips. Trim edges to within ¼ inch of center, leaving ½-inch section intact there. Unravel sides to this point. Glue 10 strips across top of head. Cut last 2 in half and glue to back of head. Gather into pigtails and tie with narrow ribbon.

Elf: Cut ribbon into 4-inch lengths. Shred, leaving ½ inch solid at top end.

Hair: Curl 22 strips over scissors' blade and glue around head, just touching hat, for one elf. For the other, glue 9 strips around head, just touching hat. Moustache: completely shred one strip, twist in middle and glue to face. Beard: Curl 4 strips over scissors blade and glue under mouth.

Second row

To fringe gift-wrapping ribbon, tape one end firmly to table surface and slit ribbon with straight pin. Leave ½ inch solid at one end.

Hair: Cut 6 7-inch lengths of ribbon. Slit each piece completely to make 3 strips. Strip 2 inches at each end into finer strips and curl over scissors' blade. Glue strips to crown of head, overlapping at angles. Cut some strips in half to fill in bare areas. Use 1 short piece for bangs. Trim bangs to desired length.

Third row

Yarn hair: Glue coil of yarn to back of head as in third drawing. Tape and pin 3 strands of yarn to table and plait. Tie ends with narrow ribbon. Fluff ends of pigtails. Glue around face in front of coil.

Fourth row

Woman, hair: Spiral head with yarn, pinning and gluing in place. Continue the spiral until it circles the head around the face, leaving the neck free. Make a smaller spiral and glue to center of head for top-knot.

Pull out cross threads.

Shred ribbon, leaving ½" solid at top.

HOLY FAMILY

ELVES

Fringe ribbon with pin.

Curl over scissors.

YARN LADY

Glue to head. Overlap at angles. Cut bangs.

Lay braided yarn around face. Tie with ribbon.

REAR VIEW

Wrap head with yarn, gluing in place.

WOMAN

Glue spiral top-knot.

CLOWN

Glue strips of yarn.

MAN

Snip small pieces of yarn. Glue to face.

Clown, hair: Cut 8 or more varying lengths of thick yarn, such as gift-wrapping. Tie in center with thread and glue to top of head. Cut bangs in front. Glue extra clippings to top of head.

Man, hair: Use same heavy yarn as for clown. Glue short strands to forehead for bangs. Cut 8 or more strands of yarn and tie in center with thread. Glue to center of head. Spread hair to cover bangs and ears. Glue to sides of head above the earline. Moustache: Glue short strand to face above mouth. Beard: Glue 6 strands to face. When glue is dry, trim to desired length.

To hang objects on nylon fishing line & transparent thread

29. Read the directions that come with the line. Nylon line or thread should be looped twice over itself for each turn of a knot so that it will hold. Knot the top end of the line in a large loop to hang object.

To copy patterns free-hand

30. To draw free-hand, study forms and reduce them to simple, geometric shapes. In this example, note that body, trousers, and feet are all made of figure eights. The head is an oval. The arms are C-shaped on the outside and approximately right-angled on the inside.

31. Use needle or push pin to punch holes in egg. In the center of the large end, make a circle of holes $\frac{1}{8}$ inch wide for decorated eggs and $\frac{1}{4}$ inch wide for lighted eggs, to go on tree. Punch a single, slightly enlarged hole in the center of the narrow end. Remove circles of shell and membrane formed by holes. Pierce inner membrane that encloses the albumen and enlarge the hole to the size of the one in the shell. Hold egg over bowl, shake egg or blow through hole to empty. Save contents for cooking. Wash out inside of egg and wipe off outside with liquid dishwasher detergent to remove any grease. Rinse well, drain until thoroughly dry.

To make shell stronger, mix a solution of 2 parts Sobo glue and 1 part water; place $\frac{1}{2}$ teaspoon or more of mixture in egg with eye dropper. Hold fingers over holes and shake vigorously to coat entire interior of egg. Shake out excess, drain and allow egg to dry thoroughly. Store shells in egg carton or plastic box.

To blow eggs

32. Save broken shells from cooking. Wash and remove membrane from inside. If soft boiled, soak before removing. Pieces of the side of the shell will be more useful than those from the end. Store in small drawers or plastic boxes.

To prepare egg shells for mosaics

Group Work

Many of the projects can be made by groups for parties of their own or for sale at bazaars and fairs to raise money. The organization of group work will vary greatly depending on the number of workers; the variety of designs that will be produced; the number of items that will be made in quantity; and the time available to complete the job. One group may meet for an afternoon or evening once a week throughout the winter. Another may devote every afternoon to a project for a single week. A family project can be arranged on a hit or miss schedule, whenever the members can gather with a little time for it. Many family Christmas projects are made in this way.

But regardless of the nature of the group and the projects, careful planning is necessary. Read through the directions for the project several times, until you are thoroughly familiar with the procedure, techniques, equipment, tools, and supplies. Be sure that everything you will need is available.

Analyze the costs and accommodate them to the group's budget. If this is a project to raise money, be certain that the items can be made and sold at a profit. Take to heart the words of the good soul who, when asked what her group did with the money it made from its annual sale, replied, "Why, we buy the materials to make the things for next year's sale!" Perpetual motion perhaps, but it scarcely puts money in the treasury.

If items are being made for sale, particularly by a group of mixed geographic, social, ethnic, or economic levels, keep a firm control over taste and styling. Know your market's level of sophistication and taste as well as your group's, particularly if they vary. Arrange that items are styled for the market, not for the group. Variations in color taste can easily get out of bounds. One man's kitsch is certainly another's camp, but be sure your customers will appreciate camp. Kitsch has a limited sale. For a successful bazaar or fair it is better if neither is in evidence.

Break down each step of the directions into its component parts; some are more detailed than others. Decide how each step can be handled most efficiently: by one person doing the complete job or by several people, each doing a part of it.

For turning out large quantities of a single item, set up a work area that will accommodate an assembly-line production. See that all supplies are at hand and within easy reach of each worker or on a nearby "buffet table" where the individual can pick up what she needs. Be sure there are enough tools. If a number of people will be using the same tool continuously, or repeatedly, try to provide one for each person. Less frequently used tools can be shared by several workers. One occasionally used piece of equipment may suffice for the entire group.

Assemble the group at the tables, explain the nature of the project, read the directions to them and assign jobs. If this is an assembly-line item, demonstrate how the object should be made. Supervise the group as it makes the first item and continue until everyone is familiar with the procedure.

For a single project of different pieces such as a castle or the spool village, you can assign the more complicated steps to 1 or 2 people to work out together while others are making the village trees on an assembly line. The construction of a core for a building had better be done by one individual, one who thoroughly understands her assignment before she begins.

For all types of work—assembly line, joint or individual—it is helpful if you know your people well enough to assign jobs to those best qualified to perform them. Tactfully arrange that congenial people work together— more will be accomplished with less friction.

If your group includes people seriously limited by age or handicapped physically or emotionally, be careful to assess their abilities and act accordingly. They might be termed the "bandage rollers"; their limitations restrict them to the repeated performance of a few simple tasks year in and year out. They are happy performing these and are upset by a major change. They are useful, however, and are often good workers. Occasionally you may be hard put to find something simple enough to keep them busy. Bear in mind at such times that their cheerful drudgery relieves others for more demanding jobs.

Other elderly or handicapped members will present a different problem. While willing, capable or even gifted, they may be unable to work except for short periods. They may not be able to come to many or any meetings, either because they lack transportation or because their health will not permit it. They want and are able to do work at home. Arrange that they have work to take with them or that can be sent to them. You will have both the use of their talents and the knowledge that you have given them a feeling of participation in the group's activities.

When working with young people, keep in mind the level of skill you are apt to find in each age group. Assign tasks that are not beyond the skill of the individuals, but that are challenging enough to keep them interested and to give them satisfaction in their accomplishments. Be sure that the work is fun.

PROJECTS I

*Holiday Decorations
for Parties, Christmas,
Valentine's Day,
and Easter*

CHRISTMAS TREE GIFT PACKAGES

For 2-dimensional tree patterns, fold a sheet of paper in half lengthwise. Roughly draw outline of half a tree on it. Cut out free-hand and unfold.

Cone Tree Pattern

MATERIALS

green construction paper	ribbon
small iridescent ball	fine wire
double-stick and magic mending tapes	Uhu glue

Pattern

1. Follow diagram opposite. Draw concentric semicircles with a compass. Divide into 12 equal pie-shape segments. (Use radius of outer semicircle to divide it into thirds. Divide each third in half and these also in half.) Draw right angle V's at points indicated in diagram.

To cut V's and make cone

2. Cut out V's with razor blade. Use a darning needle to punch a hole near point of each V. Score top lines and fold triangles up.
   Curl semicircle to form cone. Secure overlap with double-stick and magic mending tape.

Bows and balls

3. Thread small iridescent balls on fine wire. Run wire through holes, twist and spread ends to hold ornaments in place. Make bows and glue in place.

Package

4. Wrap gift box in fiery red paper before placing under cone.

Reprinted from *Seventeen*

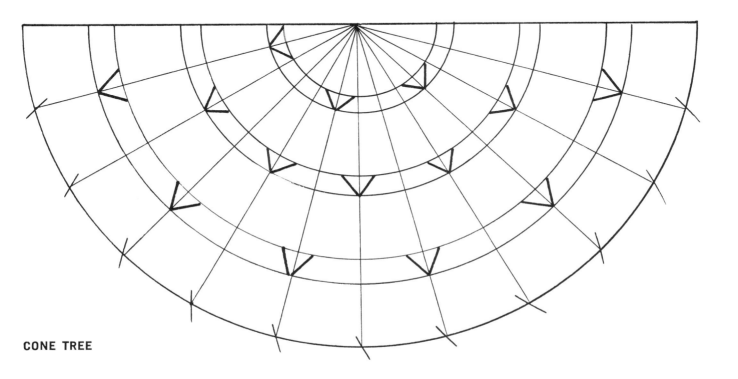

CONE TREE

3-Dimensional Tree

MATERIALS

square box	notarial seals
green construction paper	plastic tape
Styrofoam ball	small iridescent ball
knitting needle	Uhu glue

Pattern

1. Follow diagram below. Use a compass to draw 2 concentric circles and to divide them into 8 equal parts. Cut along alternate (solid) lines from outer to inner circle. Score on dotted lines.

2. Cut out octagonal. Fold up on dotted lines and fringe parallel to outer edges. Curl tips of branches down by carefully pulling them between finger and thumb. Make 5 sets of these branches.

Tree trunk

3. Punch hole in center of boxtop. Cut Styrofoam ball in half. Punch hole through center of it and the centers of the 5 sets of branches. Run knitting needle up through boxtop, balls, and branches. Use Uhu glue to glue each in place. Glue small iridescent ball to tip of needle.

4. Decorate box with large notarial seal and a strip of plastic tape around the edge of top.

Reprinted from *Seventeen*

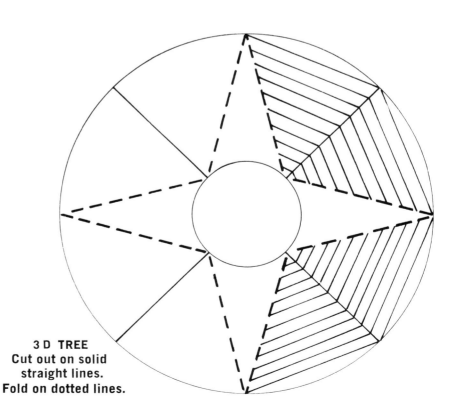

**3 D TREE
Cut out on solid
straight lines.
Fold on dotted lines.**

Stamped Wrapping Paper

MATERIALS

shelf paper	newspapers
art gum erasers	snap clothespins
ink pad	

Patterns

1. Cut a large and a small tree pattern to fit on art gum erasers. Tape pattern onto art gum. Using safety razor blade, cut around pattern and deep into art gum. Remove pattern and cut away $\frac{1}{4}$-inch depth of art gum all around tree to sides of eraser.

To use stamp

2. Practice using stamps on an ink pad and scrap paper. Note: by using stamp a second and third time without re-inking, paler trees can be printed.

3. Place plain wrapping or shelf paper on a complete, open section of newspaper, 18 or more sheets thick for padding.

For a random pattern use your stamp as fancy dictates. Vary dark and pale trees and scattered single trees with clusters. Overlap some trees, putting the paler trees behind the darker to suggest distance.

For a formal pattern draw a grid of light pencil lines on paper to use as guides for printing.

Hang paper with clothespins from line to dry overnight.

Reprinted from *Seventeen*

2-Dimensional Fold-up Tree

MATERIALS

shallow oblong box   rubber cement
colored paper   Uhu glue
2-ply bristol board   notarial seals

To cover top   1. Cut a rectangle of colored paper 1 inch smaller on all sides than top of box. Cement to box top; be sure that it adheres over entire surface (see page 28, item 24).

Tree   2. Cut rectangle of 2-ply bristol board the size of boxtop. Make pattern for tree and trace on back of board. Cut out solid lines with safety razor blade or X-acto knife. Score and fold on dotted line, as below.

3. Glue outside edge of bristol-board rectangle to boxtop. Decorate tree with 2 notarial seals, one on top of another. Glue to each other and tree with Uhu.

4. Before delivering gift, fold tree upright and bend triangle back to support it.

Reprinted from *Seventeen*

Cut out on solid lines.
Score and fold on dotted lines.

Cylinder Box

MATERIALS

oatmeal box
gift-wrapping paper
adhesive-backed felt or plastic
   (cushion-all Con-Tact)

labels
signal dots
gum-backed stars

To cover box

1. Cement circle of paper to top of oatmeal box. Cut circle ½ inch wider than boxtop so that it projects beyond it ¼ inch all around. Fringe projection into points and cement to side of box.

Cut strip of paper the depth of the box and cement paper around it.

Trees

2. Cut trees from adhesive-backed felt or plastic. Decorate trees with labels, signal dots, and stars, glued in place. Cut diamond shape finial from a large star.

Flat Ornamental Tree

MATERIALS

box
deep, brightly colored paper
self-adhesive round and oval labels

signal dots
beauty marks
gum-backed stars

To cover box

1. Wrap box in deep, brightly colored paper.

Tree

2. Cut tree from contrasting paper and decorate with ornaments made of self-adhesive round and oval labels cut out with paper punches, signal dots, beauty marks, and stars.

To attach

3. Attach to boxtop with double-stick tape. Allow edges of branches to remain loose to suggest 3 dimensions. Secure tips of branches with ornaments.

2-DIMENSIONAL CHRISTMAS TREE

MATERIALS

3 x 4-foot plywood ¼ inch	brown wrapping paper
Con-Tact plastic:	white shelf paper
green cushion-all	masking tape
red brick	map tacks
red	staples
stained glass	large gum-backed paper star
transparent frosty	light cardboard
metallic tape	Uhu glue

Pattern

1. Trace pattern (see page 45) and enlarge by squares, page 24, item 12 or cut your own pattern page 27, item 19 from brown paper. Note that each 1-inch square should be enlarged to a 6-inch square. Be sure to keep trunk thick enough not to break.

To cut out

2. Trace around pattern on plywood and cut out.

To cover

3. Cover tree with green cushion-all, trunk with red, tub with red brick, and make border of metallic tape.

Chains

4. Mount frosty and stained glass on shelf paper and cut into long arcs; each will cross tree in one sweep. Fold each arc over on itself several times and cut chains as you would paper dolls. Glue chains in place. Decorate frosty chains with bits of stained glass.

Round baubles

5. Use pinking or scallop shears to cut out circles from stained glass mounted on paper. Attach to branches with map tacks.

Snowflakes

6. Cut red flakes from red mounted on white paper, white from frosty mounted on paper. Fold a square diagonally in half (see diagrams, opposite page), then into thirds, by folding both points in over center. Cut ends

Photograph: Ralph Tornberg, Courtesy of Con-Tact® plastic

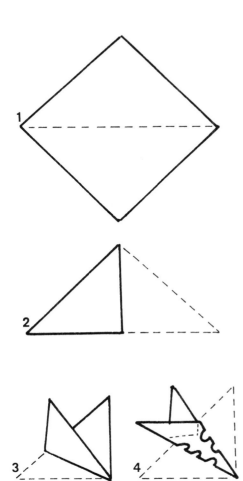

1

2

3

4

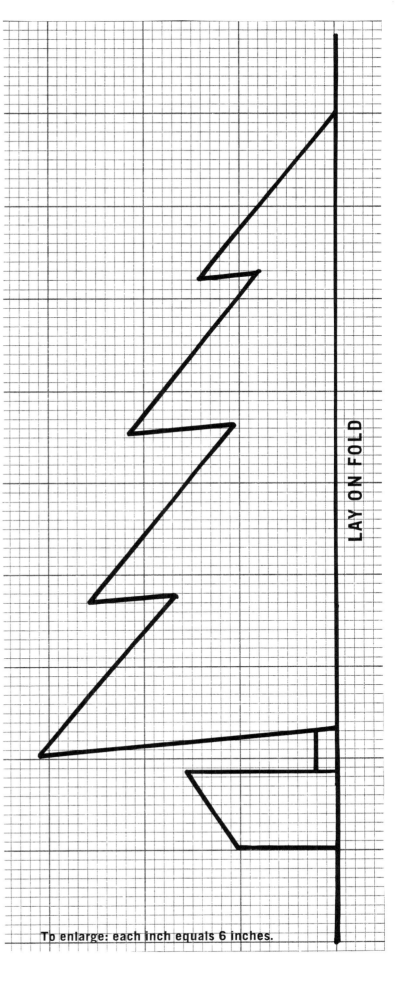

LAY ON FOLD

To enlarge: each inch equals 6 inches.

into points and notch sides with scissors and paper punches. Open and attach with glue and map tacks.

Diamonds *7.* Cut long diamonds from metallic tape and press in place.
Sunburst *8.* Cut an 8 x 11-inch rectangle from frosty mounted on paper and pleat horizontally. Staple across center of pleats, cut ends into long points, and notch folded sides with scissors. Open both ends into fans until outer edges meet. Staple ends together. Attach with glue and map tacks.

Star *9.* Draw 5-pointed star inside 7-inch radius circle on back of stained glass. See items 16 and 17, page 26.

Do not remove backing. Cut out circle. Cut along lines from edge of circle to each V.

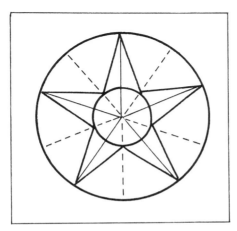 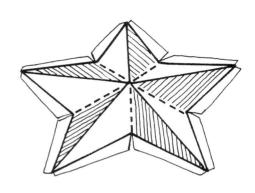

Cut long triangles of cardboard to fit into 4 of these pockets. Overlap triangle bases and glue together.

To attach tree Cut a strip of cardboard 1¾ wide and 18 inches long. Point end and
to wall slip into fifth pocket. Glue in place. Slip tip of tree behind this strip and the overlapped cardboard in center. Tape strip to back of tree.

Attach tree to wall with metal cleats.

ALTERNATES

Ornaments Omit plywood and apply tree directly to painted wall. Do *not* apply over wallpaper.

Use the snowflakes, baubles, sunburst, and star separately as ornaments on any 3-dimensional tree. Cover both sides of the paper with Con-Tact so that they can be viewed from both sides. Hang with heavy thread or nylon line or thread (see item 29, General Directions, page 32).

CHRISTMAS TREE ORNAMENTS

(See color plate 3.)

MATERIALS

clear plastic electric-
   typewriter ribbon spools
single and double ruffling
thread
notarial seals
imitation marabou or long-
   haired fur
roof tins
jumbo curtain-fringe balls
beads
boutique-trim rhinestone daisies
wide-tinsel garland

pull tabs
rhinestones
soutache braid
button and carpet thread or
    nylon thread or fishing line
cellophane-ruffled toothpicks
gummed reinforcements for
   notebooks
flitter
rubber cement
Uhu glue

1. Wash spools in warm soapy water, rinse, and dry.

To clean spools

2. Measure and cut a length of garland to fit inside spool. Run a line of glue down middle of garland. Use a toothpick to push garland against center of spool. Rotate spool as you work to spread garland evenly. Glue notarial seal to center of each side. Run thread or fishing line through hole in center of spool and knot ends together to hang (see page 32, item 29).

Tinsel ornament

3. Cover outside of spool with rubber cement and sprinkle with flitter. Follow directions in step 2 to glue marabou inside spool. Hang with red soutache braid.

Marabou ornament

4. Gather ruffling tightly on white thread. Make long enough to fit around center of spool and knot thread before cutting ruffling. Run line of glue along edge of ruffling and follow directions in step 2 to glue ruffling inside of spool. Overlap ends and sew edges together. Decorate centers with notarial seals.

Two ruffled ornaments

Ruffled toothpick ornament

5. Glue ruffled toothpicks to one side of spool. When glue has dried, turn spool over and glue picks to other side. Glue a large white and a small black gummed reinforcement over center of each side.

Roof tin and curtain-ball ornament

6. Glue 4 roof tins to each side of spool. Arrange so that half of each tin projects beyond edge of spool. Between tins, glue fringe balls. Glue rhinestone daisies in center of each tin.

Pull-tab ornaments

7. Leave tab ends curled and twisted. Glue the circular ends of 4 tabs to each side of spool. Arrange so that projecting ends alternate on one side and then the other, as in photograph. Glue rhinestones in center of circular ends, and beads between them.

IRIDESCENT BALLS

MATERIALS

3-inch iridescent balls   Uhu glue
metallic ribbon

Ornament A

1. Crisscross 2 24-inch-length ribbons and glue to ball. Loop ends and glue to neck of ball.

Cut 6 7-inch lengths of ribbon. Cut away edges to within ½ inch of end. Unravel, leaving ½-inch solid area at end (see item 28, top row, page 30). Glue 3 of these under each of 2 loops.

Ornament B

2. Cut 3 lengths of ribbon 24 inches long. Unravel to within 3 inches of center, leaving 6 inches solid. Fold this 6 inches in half lengthwise and iron edge. Crisscross around neck of ball. Curl unraveled ends with scissors blade.

Ornament C

3. Cut 6-inch length of ribbon. Glue center to bottom of ball. Crease 1 inch from center on both sides. Overlap ends and glue to center.

4. Cut 4 7-inch lengths of ribbon. Unravel, leaving ½ inch solid at one end. Glue these ends to center of bow.

Ornament D

5. Make loops as for C on each side of ball. Unravel and curl 6 7-inch lengths of ribbon. Curl over scissors blade. Glue solid ends under loops.

Courtesy of NORCROSS DESIGN STUDIOS

(See color plate 2.) # SPOOL CHRISTMAS TREE ORNAMENTS

These can be hung on the tree, from the ceiling, or on long threads or lines from the ceiling over the dinner table.

MATERIALS

empty spools	¼-inch heavy-duty sisal rope
large wooden play beads	adhesive spray
dressmaker's findings:	Saran wrap
ruffling	fine flitter
woven ribbons	foil chocolate cups
gold and colored braids	enamel paint
Venice-lace edging	felt-tipped marking pens
straight pins	Sobo glue
gold and silver beads	Uhu glue
nylon thread or fishline	

To paint beads

1. Paint beads if they are worn or chipped.

To wash foil cups

2. Wash chocolate cups in hot suds, rinse and allow to dry (see item 6, page 21).

To prepare spools

3. Remove labels from ends of spools. Spools for carpet thread are usually colored. They can be retouched with markers. Bare spools can be completely colored or if their sides are to be covered with ribbon, the ends only should be colored.

To decorate

4. Use Sobo glue to attach fabrics. Glue ribbon and braids around sides of spools. Apply glue to braids and ribbon and wait until it is tacky before pressing them onto spools. Trim edges of spools with braids and Venice-lace edging. Use pins to hold ends of tape and ribbons together while glue dries.

To attach play beads

5. When the glued fabrics have dried, attach beads to ends of spools with Uhu glue.

To hang

6. Hang ornaments on nylon thread or fishline. See item 29, page 32. Read the directions that come with the line. Nylon line should be looped twice over itself for each turn of a knot so that it will hold. Knot the top end of the line in a large loop to hang ornament.

Ornament A

7. Glue foil circles from E to end of spool. Glue ribbon around spool and gold edging at either end of it.

Insert line through small bead; knot line around it. Punch hole in center of foil cup and insert line. Drop cup down to rest on bead. Repeat for second and third cups. Add fourth bead and run line through spool. Loop and knot end to hang.

Ornament B

8. Glue ribbon around spool and ruffling at edges of ribbon. Overlap ruffling about ⅜ inch. Glue flat beads to either end of spool. Run line through silver bead and hang as for ornament A.

Ornament C   9. Glue gold braid around spool and narrower green braid around its top and bottom edges. Glue round play beads to each end.

Flatten 4 foil cups. Use Uhu to glue centers back to back to make 2 flat circles. Cut fringe around edges. Punch 2 holes in center of each circle.

Knot end of line and insert line through holes in one circle. Slip line twice through a silver bead and knot around it. Put line through spool and knot around a second silver bead at top. Knot line below second foil circle and run through holes in circle. Put drops of Uhu between silver beads and ornament. When glue is tacky, press beads and ornament together. Lay ornament on side and allow glue to dry overnight.

Ornament D   10. Glue ribbon around center of spool and braid around edges. Glue play beads to ends of spools.

Run a piece of rope through bead and knot tightly at either end, leaving 6 inches at bottom and a shorter length at top. Cut top piece off above knot. Open bottom piece and unravel to loosen fringe for tassel. Dip in water and pull strands straight. Dry overnight.

Fluff out tassel. Wrap ornament carefully in Saran wrap. Spray tassel with adhesive and sprinkle with flitter. Repeat on knot at top. Run nylon thread under top knot and tie ends together to hang.

Ornament E   11. Glue ribbon around spool and red Venice-lace edging around top and bottom. Flatten 2 foil cups with a rolling pin and cut a circle from the center of each cup. Lay circles aside and save for ornament A. Roll remaining edges of cups around finger to form spirals. Cut points at end. Insert one point of each spiral into opposite ends of spool and glue with Uhu. Lay ornament on side while glue dries.

Tie line through a silver bead before running line through spool and top spiral. Wedge pieces of foil around line in top of hole so that spool will hang straight.

Ornament F   12. Glue braid around Styrofoam spool and glue flat play beads at either end.

Thread spool with rope and knot as above, leaving 2 inches above knot on top. Open both ends and unravel but do not wet. Leave curly and trim bottom tassel loosely at sides so that it is shaped to a point. Wrap in Saran wrap as above. Spray with adhesive and sprinkle lightly with flitter. Hang as above.

ELVES

MATERIALS

gift-wrapping foil paper	button or carpet thread
gift-wrapping metallic ribbon	yellow construction paper
gift-wrapping metallic cord	thin pipe cleaners
iridescent balls	rubber cement
signal dots	Uhu glue

Tunic

1. Cut out 2 semicircles of foil paper with $6\frac{5}{8}$-inch radii. Fold each into quarters and open as in diagram 1 page 55. Refold as in diagrams 2 and 3.

2. Trace pattern. Lay on fold AD as in diagram 4 and cut out. Slit seams at top to dotted line. Fold under on dotted lines.

3. Glue edges of sides of tunic and seams of undersleeve together. (Keep inside of sleeves hollow.) Overlap back and glue. Sharpen crease AD.

4. Cut 4 strips, 7 inches long, of metallic ribbon. Cut off edges to $\frac{1}{2}$ inch of end and unravel, leaving $\frac{1}{2}$ inch solid at top end. Glue solid ends to top front of tunic.

Collar

5. Trace pattern and cut out. Cut out lower edge with pinking shears or scallop shears. Glue to top of tunic. Overlap and glue at back.

Arms

6. Cut 5-inch length of pipe cleaner for each arm. Remove string from metallic cord; slip over pipe cleaner for arm. Insert arms into sleeves and glue to shoulders.

Hands

7. Trace pattern and cut 2 hands for each arm. Place one hand under and one over end of arm and glue together.

Legs

8. Cement 2 sheets of foil paper back to back. Trace pattern for legs and cut out 2 for each figure.

Boots

9. Trace pattern and cut out 2 for each leg. Place on each side of foot and glue together.

To attach

10. Glue one leg to the underside of the front of tunic and one to the underside of the back.

Face   11. When figure is finished, head will hang from wire loop in ball. So make face on ball with wire loop at top.

Glue signal-dot eyes to face.

12. Cut a strip of construction paper $\frac{3}{8}$ x $1\frac{1}{2}$ inches, roll, and glue into a circle. Glue to ball for nose.

13. Remove string from metallic cord. Iron flat. Cut $\frac{1}{2}$-inch length. Curve between thumb and forefinger. Glue in place for mouth.

14. Cut circles of 2 and $3\frac{3}{8}$-inch radii for hats. Use scallop or pinking shears to cut out one. Slit to centers; roll into cones. Overlap back and glue.

Hair   15. See item 28, top row, page 30. Cut metallic ribbon in $4\frac{1}{4}$-inch lengths. Unravel, leaving $\frac{1}{2}$ inch solid at top end.

16. Curl 22 strips of these over scissors blade and glue around head just below hat. Glue 9 strips, uncurled, around other head.

Moustache and beard   17. Completely unravel 1 strip of ribbon, twist in middle, and glue to face. Make beard of 4 curled strips of unraveled ribbon, a solid $\frac{1}{2}$-inch width at ends.

To assemble   18. Tie thread to ball and run threads through point of hat. Glue hat to head. Tie loop at end of thread to hang.

19. Glue folds at top of tunic to head.

Courtesy of NORCROSS DESIGN STUDIOS

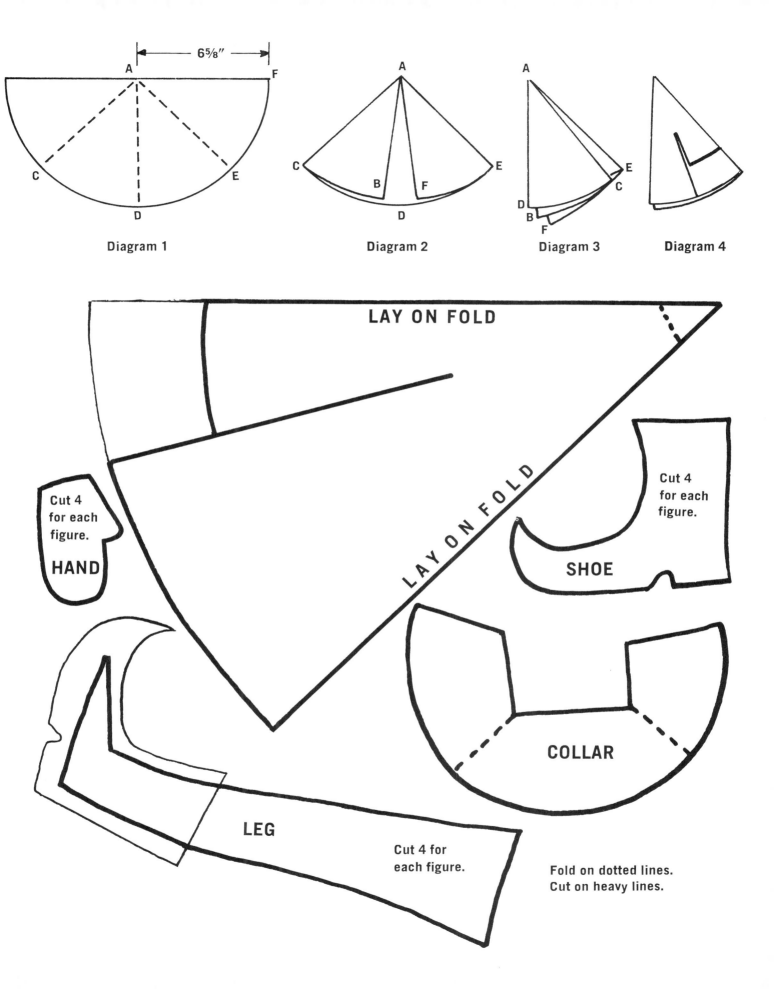

Diagram 1

Diagram 2

Diagram 3

Diagram 4

6⅝″

A F

C E

D

A

C E

B F

D

A

C

D E

B

F

A

LAY ON FOLD

LAY ON FOLD

Cut 4 for each figure.

HAND

Cut 4 for each figure.

SHOE

COLLAR

LEG

Cut 4 for each figure.

Fold on dotted lines.
Cut on heavy lines.

YARN LADIES

MATERIALS

gift-wrapping yarn
gift-wrapping metallic and
    glossy ribbon
gift-wrapping metallic cord
Styrofoam eggs, 2 inches long
Styrofoam balls, 1¼- and
    2-inch diameter
poster paints

beads
button or carpet thread to
    match yarns
felt-tipped marking pens
Sobo glue
6-inch straight upholstery
    needle

Head   1. Paint eggs and allow to dry overnight. Draw features with marking pens.

Hair   2. See item 28, second row, page 30. For each head, cut 7-inch lengths of glossy ribbon. Slit each length into 3 strips. Slit 2 inches at each end and curl over scissors blade. Glue strips to crown of head, overlapping at angles. Cut some strips in half to fit over bare areas. Cut one strip into short lengths for bangs. Trim hair and bangs as desired.

Bow   3. Make a bow of metallic ribbon and glue on top of head.

Bodice   4. For each figure, cut 8 lengths of metallic ribbon 3½ inches long (color to match skirt). Run line of glue down center of each strip and, spacing evenly, glue to 2-inch ball. Cut 8 more of contrasting color and glue, covering areas between first 8.

Skirt   5. Cut 24 lengths of yarn 12 inches long. Arrange in a bundle. Cut a 36-inch length of carpet thread. Tie and knot center of thread around center of yarn. Slip small Styrofoam ball under center of yarn and glue thread and yarn to ball. Drape yarn around ball and trim ends evenly.

Arms   6. Cut 5 lengths of yarn 7 inches long for each arm. Tie (as in skirt) with 24-inch lengths of thread. Using upholstery needle, run thread from one arm through shoulders. Knot thread from other arm to this and cut away extra thread.

Pull cotton string from inside 4 inches of metallic cord and iron flat. Cover one side with glue and wrap around arms.

7. Using upholstery needle, draw thread from skirt through body, bead, and head. Knot thread tightly at top of head to hold parts securely together. Make second knot at end of thread so that doll can be hung if desired.

Put drop of glue at top and bottom of bead. Turn head to face forward and allow to dry in position.

To assemble

(See color plate 12.) # FIGURES WITH CURTAIN-FRINGE BALL HEADS

MATERIALS

2-ply bristol board	thread
staples	toothpicks
old neckties and their linings	adhesive-backed gold braid
1-inch diameter (extra large) balls from curtain fringe	feather
	glass-headed pins
coral-colored liquid textile dye	flat decorative button
black and brown fine yarn	Sobo glue
felt	

Bodies

1. Make cone from $2\frac{1}{4}$-inch-diameter semicircle. Staple cone together.

2. Cut off narrow end of necktie. Open, remove lining, and iron both pieces flat. Glue fabric over cone. For the man, use a striped tie and be careful to run a stripe vertically down the center front of body.

Vest

3. Cut man's vest from felt as in C, and glue to body. His tie is cut from a white lining.

Cape

4. For the woman's cape, fold a 2-inch square of lining in half, A. Shape as in B and glue to figure along front edges and down center back. Edge with gold braid. Cut and attach 2 pieces of braid at throat for bow.

Heads

5. Make heads of curtain fringe balls. Either use pink balls, or dye white ones with coral liquid dye. Use $\frac{1}{4}$ teaspoon of dye to 3 cups of water and follow directions on bottle. Fluff balls occasionally as they dry.

6. Glue each ball to the end of a toothpick.

7. For eyes and nose, cut shanks from glass-headed pins $\frac{1}{4}$ inch from head. Put drop of glue on a shank and insert it into a ball.

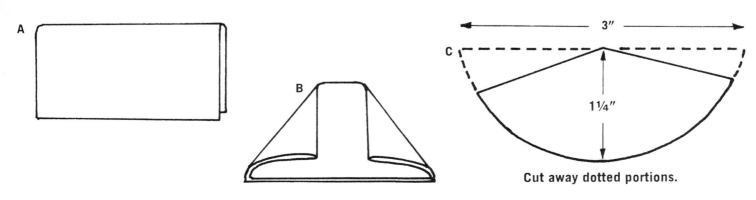

A

B

C ← 3″ →

1¼″

Cut away dotted portions.

8. Make hair and moustache of yarn.

9. Insert other end of toothpick through point of cone and secure from inside with a drop of glue.

10. Woman's bandana is a triangle $4\frac{1}{2}$ x $2\frac{3}{4}$ x $2\frac{3}{4}$ inches, glued over hair and under chin.

11. Cut purse as in diagram D; fold on dotted line. Wrap its neck with thread. Glue purse to body.

Bandana and purse

12. Man's hat is a $1\frac{1}{2}$-inch-diameter circle cut from 2 layers of felt glued together. Glue hat to head. Punch hole in center of hat and glue button over hole. Stich end of feather with drop of glue through button into hole.

Hat

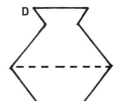

HOLY FAMILY

MATERIALS

gift-wrapping foil paper
gift-wrapping metallic and
　glossy ribbon
gift-wrapping metallic cord
small box 4 x 3 x 1½ inches
star sequins
boutique trim flowers
silver flitter
7-inch, double-pointed knitting
　needle

straight pins
Styrofoam cones 9 inches high
Styrofoam balls 1¼ and
　2½-inch diameter
2-ply bristol board
poster paint
map tacks
Sobo glue
rubber cement

Heads　　1. Paint balls and tint cheeks. Allow to dry overnight. Make eyes and noses on Mary and Joseph with map tacks; mouths of triangles of red ribbons.

Bodies　　2. For Mary and Joseph use rubber cement to cover cones with gift papers. Push points of cones into heads and glue in place. Cut Infant's body from 3-inch-long egg shape of bristol board. Remove string from inside metallic cord, iron cord flat, and glue criss-cross on body. Cut away extra cord along edges. Make slit in head and insert top of body with a drop glue.

Cape　　3. Glue parallel strips of metallic ribbon together with one strip at right angles across top edge. Allow to dry (see diagram, page 62).

Make cape pattern the shape in diagram, page 62, enlarged to 9 inches deep. Cut cape from above ribbons. Place flat edge of cape along strip of ribbon at right angle to other strips.

Pin center back of cape to back of body. Pin front edge of cape to body, letting sides flare out.

Mary's hair　　4. Cut twelve 16-inch-long strips of metallic ribbon. Trim off edges to within ¼ inch of center, leaving ½-inch section intact there. Unravel each side to this point. Glue 10 strips across top of head. Cut 2 more strips in half and glue to back of head. Gather into pigtails and tie with narrow ribbon (see diagrams, item 28, top row, page 30).

Crown

5. Make circle of 3 layers of glossy ribbon to fit around head. Use Sobo to glue ends down. Cut points in top. Glue on star sequins. Glue crown to head.

Joseph's hair and beard

6. Cut ten 6-inch-long strips of metallic ribbon. Cut off edge on each side, unravel, leaving $\frac{1}{2}$ inch intact at one end. Glue 10 to face for beard (see diagrams, item 28, top row, page 30).

Cut twenty-seven 4-inch-long strips of same ribbon. Trim edges and unravel except for $\frac{1}{2}$ inch in center of each strip. Curl 18 strips over scissors blade. Leave top of head bare and glue hair around head in 2 layers. Glue 9 more unraveled but uncurled strips in third layer beneath first 2. Fluff ends.

Prepare 2 more unraveled strips with $\frac{1}{2}$ inch intact in center. Twist together at middle and glue to head for moustache.

Courtesy of NORCROSS DESIGN STUDIOS

Staff   7. Wrap knitting needle with metallic ribbon. Unravel 6 3-inch-long strips of ribbon leaving ½ inch intact at one end. Wrap these around top of staff and glue in place. Glue flowers to it.

Halos   8. Glue 2 pieces of foil paper back to back for each halo. Use a different color for each. Make Mary's 6¼ inches, Joseph's 3½ inches, and the Infant's 1¾ inches in diameter. Cut with scallop or pinking shears.

Manger   9. Cover box with wide, glossy ribbon. Fold strip of metallic ribbon in half lengthwise and iron flat. Glue around top of box. Unravel metallic ribbon in 4-inch lengths and fill box. Place Infant in it.

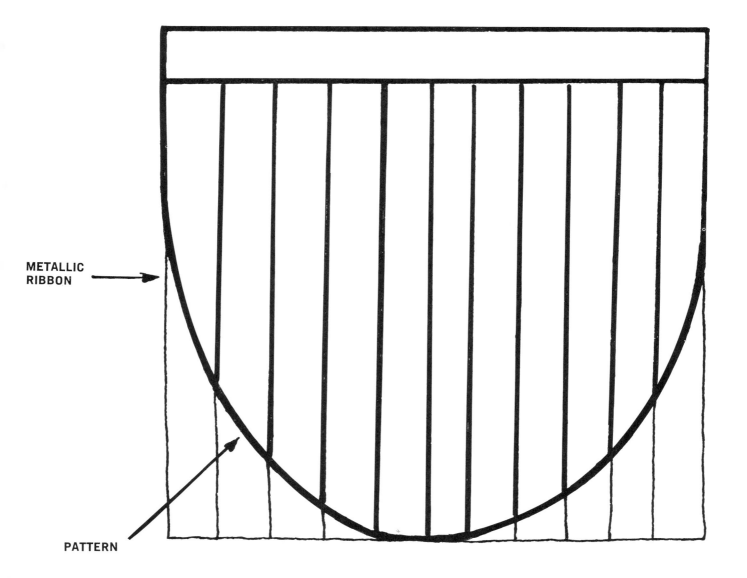

METALLIC RIBBON

PATTERN

THREE WISE MEN

MATERIALS

gift-wrapping yarn

gift-wrapping metallic cord

gift-wrapping glossy and
    metallic ribbon

gift-wrapping paper

white lightweight cardboard

felt-tipped marking pens

notarial seal

rubber cement

Uhu glue

1. Trace patterns (pages 64–65) and transfer to cardboard. Cut out figures. Color faces and draw features with marking pens.

Pattern

2. Spread glue on an area of the costume. Press yarn into glue. Use photograph as a guide to arrange the yarn in patterns. Repeat process with each area until all yarn is in place. Attach metallic cord in the same way.

Ethiopian costume

Courtesy of NORCROSS DESIGN STUDIOS

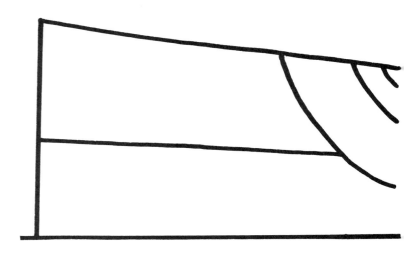

Hair Fringe 5 2½-inch lengths of black glossy ribbon (see item 28, 2nd row, page 30), leaving ¼ inch solid at one end. Glue 2 to head for hair, 1 to face for beard. Trim. Twist fifth into moustache and attach with glue. Glue crown in place.

Caucasian 3. Follow same procedure as above for costume.

Hair and beard 4. Cut 8 2½-inch lengths of metallic ribbon (see item 28, top row, page 30). Trim off edges to within ½ inch of one end. Unravel ribbon, leaving last ½ inch solid. Curl 6 lengths over scissors blade. Glue to head for hair. Glue an uncurled length to face for beard, cutting out a V in center of top edge, as in photograph. Twist last length and glue in place as moustache. Attach crown with glue.

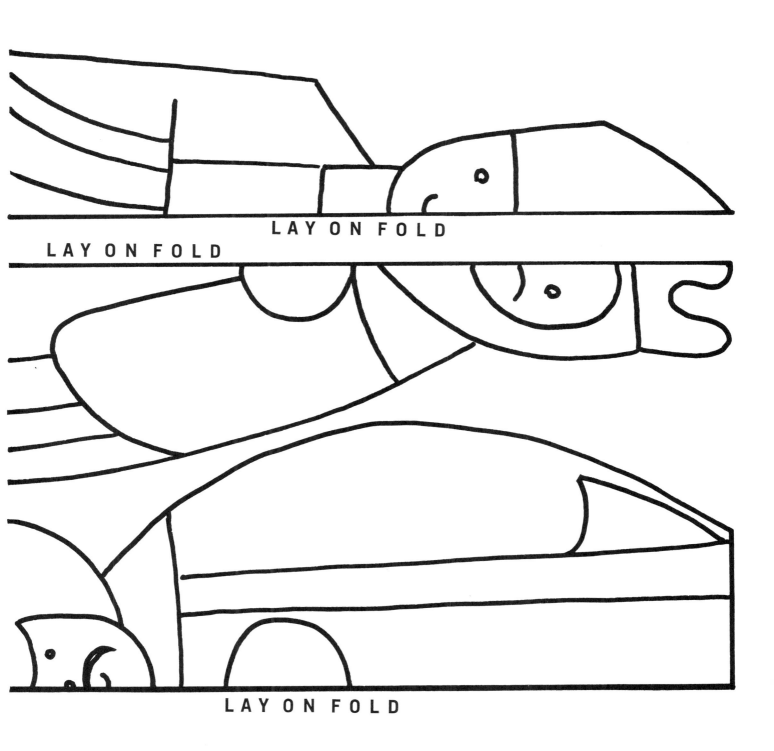

LAY ON FOLD

LAY ON FOLD

LAY ON FOLD

LAY ON FOLD

Gift   5. Form a length of metallic ribbon into a semicircle of 8 loops, as in photograph. Glue ends and folds together. Glue to figure.

Oriental   6. Follow same procedure as above for yarn.

Turban   7. Cut 4 5-inch lengths of metallic ribbon. Cut off edges and unravel, leaving $\frac{1}{2}$ inch solid in *center*. Lay 2 together, fold in center, and twist. Repeat with other 2. Glue 1 set $\frac{1}{4}$ inch below other in center of turban. Glue notarial seal over base.

To stand   8. Cut and score cardboard triangles as in diagram and glue to back of figures for support. See page 29, item 25.

PAPER AND CARDBOARD CRÈCHE

(See color plate 3.)

MATERIALS

lightweight and heavy cardboards
plain and patterned gift-
   wrapping paper
heavy colored paper
gold-embossed paper cut-outs
sequins

silver and white lace-paper
   doilies
colored pencils
cardboard box 9 x 5 x 4 inches
rubber cement
Uhu glue

1. For each figure trace patterns onto lightweight cardboard. Cut out complete silhouette ⅛ inch inside outline on top and sides, but *not* on bottom.

2. Cut out complete silhouette of figure from paper of costume's predominant color. Cement over cardboard.

3. Cut out remaining parts of figure and costume and cement in place. Add gold-embossed paper cut-outs, lace-paper doilies, and sequins.

4. Make features of slivers of paper or with colored pencils.

5. Glue scored triangles of cardboard to back of figures for them to stand upright (see diagram, item 25, page 29).

6. Cut down box to form shelter (see diagram). Reinforce walls and make roof of heavy cardboard, glued in place. Cover with colored and foil papers, cemented to cardboard.

ALTERNATE

Enlarge patterns to half or full life-size—6 inches or 1 foot to an inch. Cut from ½-inch plywood, paint with weatherproof paints, and use as crèche in outdoor display.

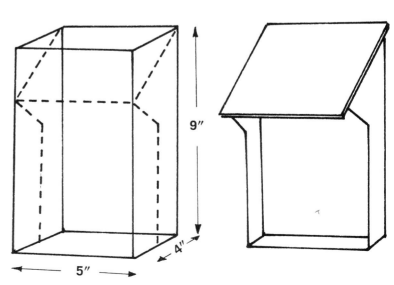

CUT-OUT CRÈCHE

MATERIALS

2-ply bristol board   magic mending and double-stick
tracing paper   tape
heavy cardboard   eraser

1. Trace patterns on tracing paper. *Reverse* and trace onto the back of the bristol board so that finished figures will face in the directions photographed (pages 74–77).   ***Patterns***

2. Note that all figures except angel have 1 or 2 perpendicular sides. From this perpendicular, extend a right triangle whose base is an extension of the figure's lower edge. Under the lower edge, draw a ¾-inch-deep flap. Both triangle and flap are included on the Madonna's pattern.   ***Flaps***

On angel, extend base line out 2 inches and connect its end with a point 2 inches up one side of skirt to form a triangle. Later trim triangle to an angle that will support figure. Make flap on lower edge of angel.

3. Place bristol board, wrong side up, on 2 layers of heavy cardboard. Use a safety razor or an X-acto knife with a No. 16 blade. Use a fresh blade for each figure. Begin with large inner openings. Place knife point in a corner, bear down and cut along each line with one stroke.   ***To cut out***

Until your hands and fingers become accustomed to the work, cut out only 2 figures each day.

4. Use a blade to cut away areas such as parts of crowns and the halos of Virgin and Child, sleeves of 2 of the Wise Men, the angel's hands and some of the eyes.   ***Large open areas***

5. Use ⅛- and ¼-inch paper punches for animals' eyes and nostrils, and decorations on costumes and crowns.   ***Paper punch holes***

6. Punch holes with needles. Prick fine holes from the rear, reverse figures, and punch larger hole through each from front.   ***Needle holes***

7. Cut tails and angel's hair and halo with embroidery scissors. On halo, fold alternate strips forward.   ***Fringes***

8. Cut long, narrow strips with square or pointed ends for hair, straw in manger, sheeps' wool of shepherds' cloaks, wool on lambs, and decorations on angel's wings.

    Pull some strips out and up, away from background, curl others over scissors blade or around a very heavy darning needle.

Strips

9. On the tall king's cape, the angel's and Madonna's robes, cut V's and score a line connecting the open ends. Fold these triangles in or out, as indicated in the photograph.

    On the Oriental king's turban, cut 4 V's one inside the other, and fold alternate triangles in or out.

Triangles and V's

10. Cut an X with a blade. Push center slightly forward. Use a paper punch to cut hole in center of some X's.

X's

11. Repair any mistakes with tape or narrow strips of bristol board.

To repair

12. Use kneaded eraser to clean backs of figures and any smudges on the fronts.

To clean

13. Score lines separating figures from triangle at sides and flaps at lower edges. Fold under.

To score flaps

14. Trim base of triangles to slight angle so that figure will be cantered imperceptively backward. Stand figure upright on flap and base of triangle. Tape base and triangle together.

To stand upright

15. Crèche can be displayed on a tier of boxes as in photograph or on a single level in a long, narrow arrangement. Use a dark background in either case. Attach flap to horizontal surface with double-stick tape. Place a lamp or spotlight either to one side or above crèche to accentuate details.

To display

16. Cut tape and press figures flat. Place figures under a sheet of tracing or tissue paper and go over them with a warm iron to remove tape. Clean off any stubborn adhesive with rubber cement thinner. Place figures between sheets of tissue paper in a shallow box. Cover and wrap with paper to keep out dust.

Storage

74

LAY ON FOLD

Prick on dotted lines.

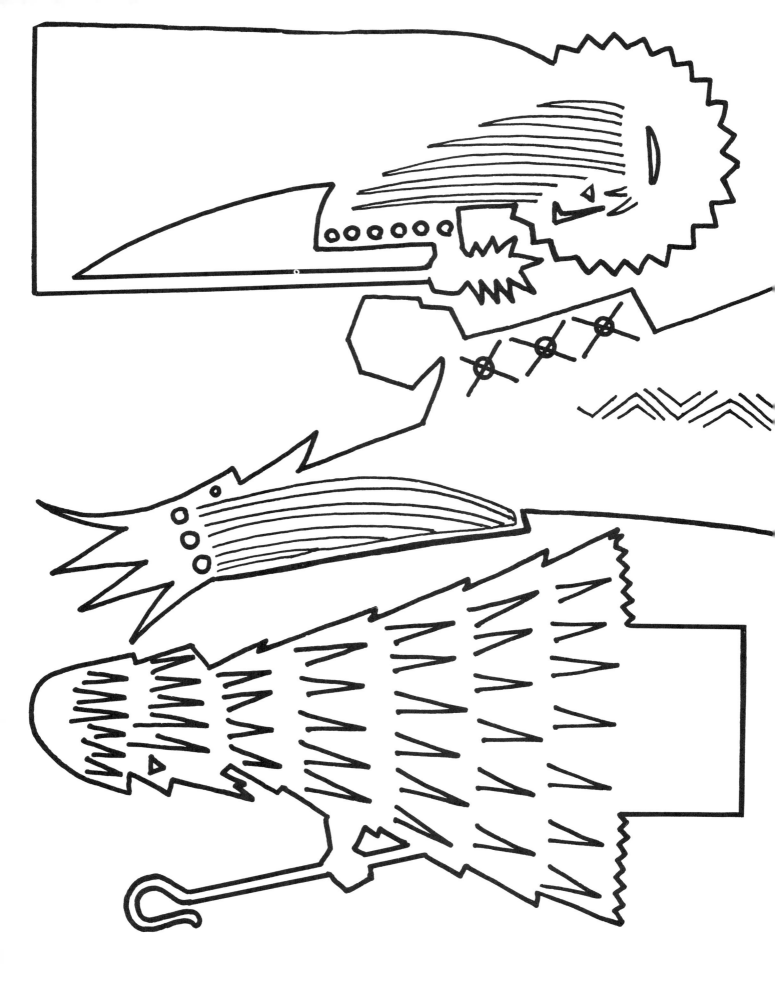

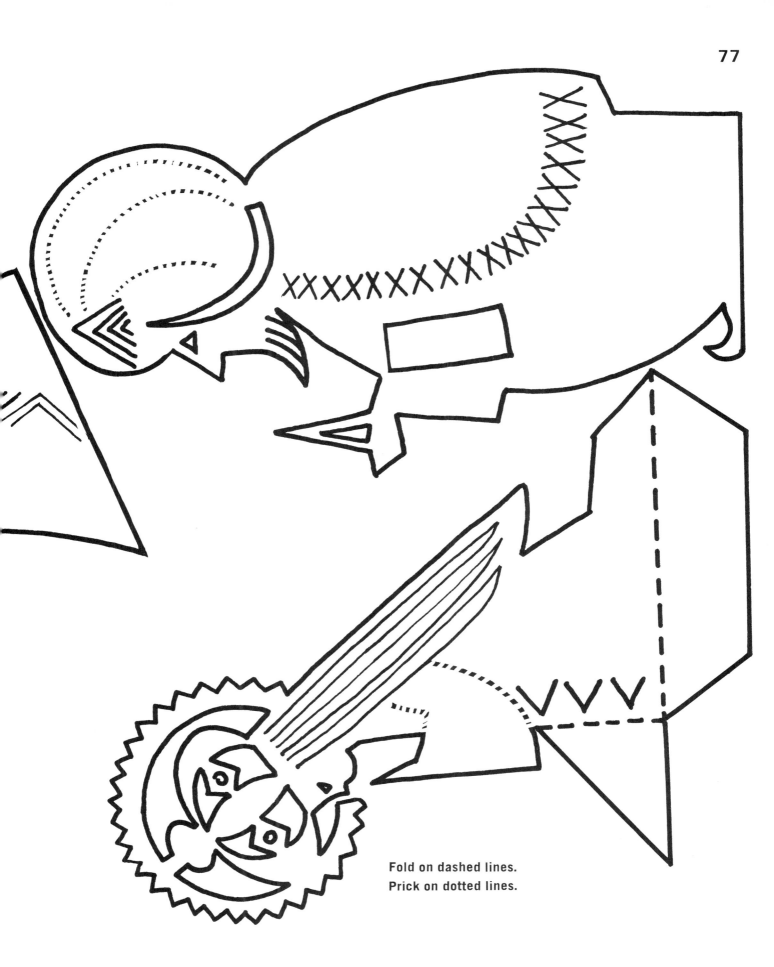

Fold on dashed lines.
Prick on dotted lines.

REINDEER AND SLED

MATERIALS

patterned foil and colored gift-
   wrapping paper
gift-wrapping metallic cord
3-ply bristol board
small pipe cleaners
gold beads

pine cone
wire coathanger
felt-tipped marking pens
gold map tacks
rubber cement
Uhu glue

Sled patterns

1. Trace pattern (pages 80–82) on board, cut out, and score dotted lines.

To cover

2. Cement patterned foil paper over all inside areas of sled, as in photograph. Cement colored paper over outside parts of sled. Punch holes at points N, O, P, and Q. Fold on dotted lines.

To assemble

3. Curl ends of part C by gently pulling them over the flat side of a table knife. Match points W, X, Y, and Z in parts A, B, and C. Glue A, B, and C together. Fold flaps T and U at right angles to the brace V. Glue flap S to back of runner R.

Top braces

4. Remove string from inside metallic cord and slip over 2 pipe cleaners. Insert ends of pipe cleaners in holes of O and N. Cut cleaners so that opposite ends will fit into holes P and Q and hold sides of sled upright. Leave $\frac{1}{4}$ inch projecting from holes at both ends. Glue gold beads over all 4 ends, as in photograph.

Cord trimming

5. Glue metallic cord around all edges of sled except the runners. See photograph.

Reindeer

6. Cement colored paper over both sides of a piece of board slightly larger than head. Trace pattern onto it and cut out.

7. Draw eyes and color exposed edges of board with marking pens.

To attach

8. Use a sharp knife or safety razor blade and *carefully* cut slit in pine cone. Insert neck into slit with a drop of glue (see page 83).

9. Cut 4 pieces of wire of equal length from coathanger. At one end of each, bend a foot at right angles to leg.

Legs

10. Push legs into pine cone and glue in place. Before glue sets, adjust legs to balance reindeer. Then place it upside down in a glass and apply a liberal amount of glue to area where leg joins cone. Let dry overnight.

To attach legs

11. Remove string from metallic cord, iron flat, and glue to head for bridle, as in photograph.

Bridle

12. Leave string in a longer length of cord and glue ends to bridle for reins. Glue gold map tack into each side over joint.

Reins

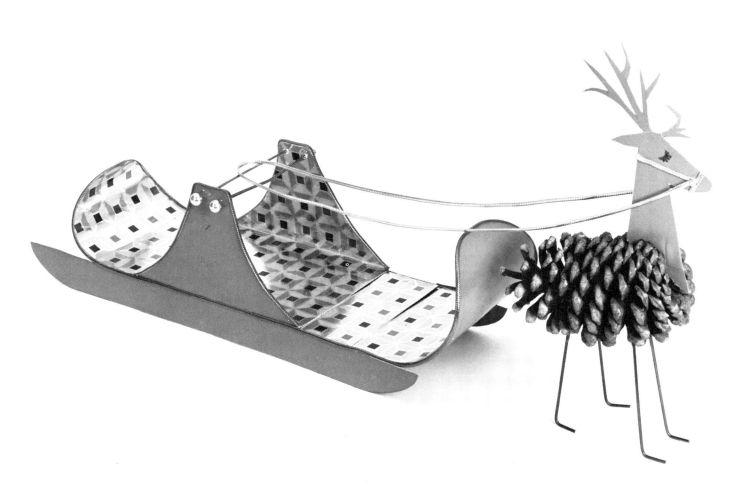

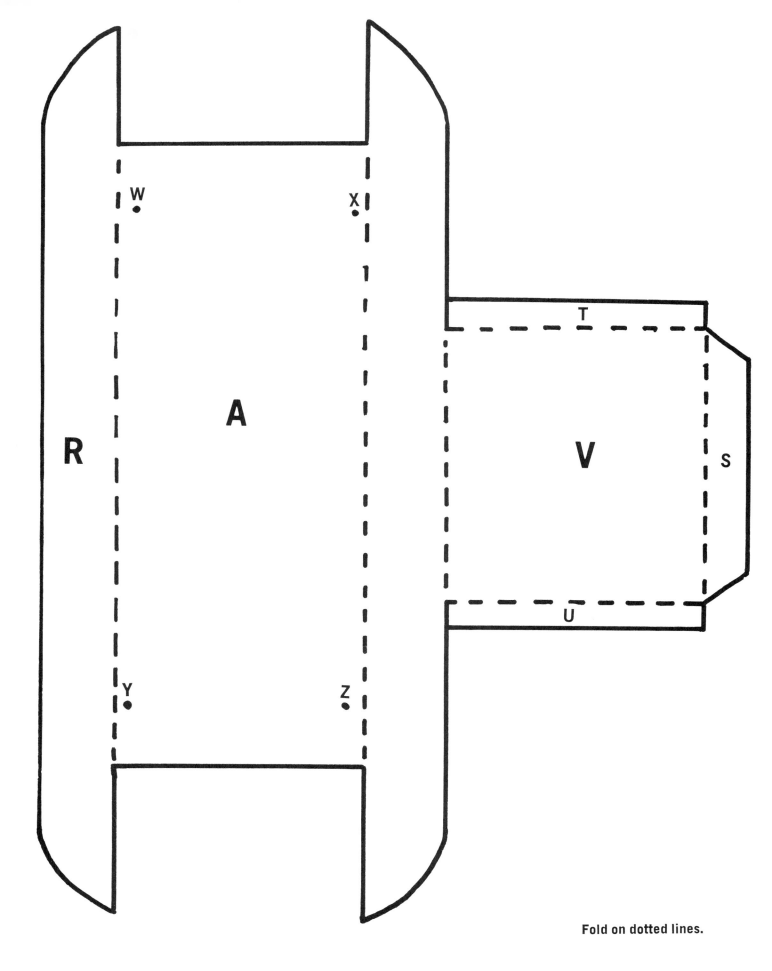

Fold on dotted lines.

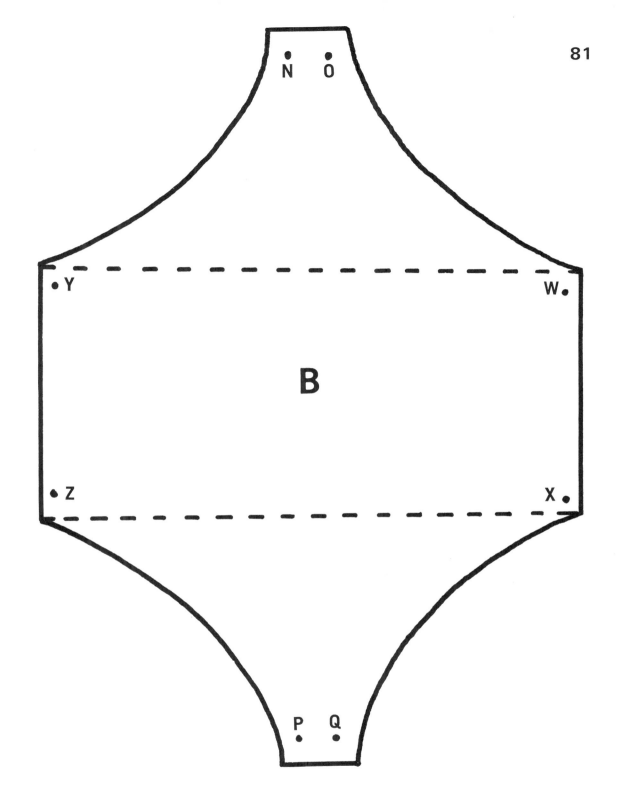

Fold on dotted lines.

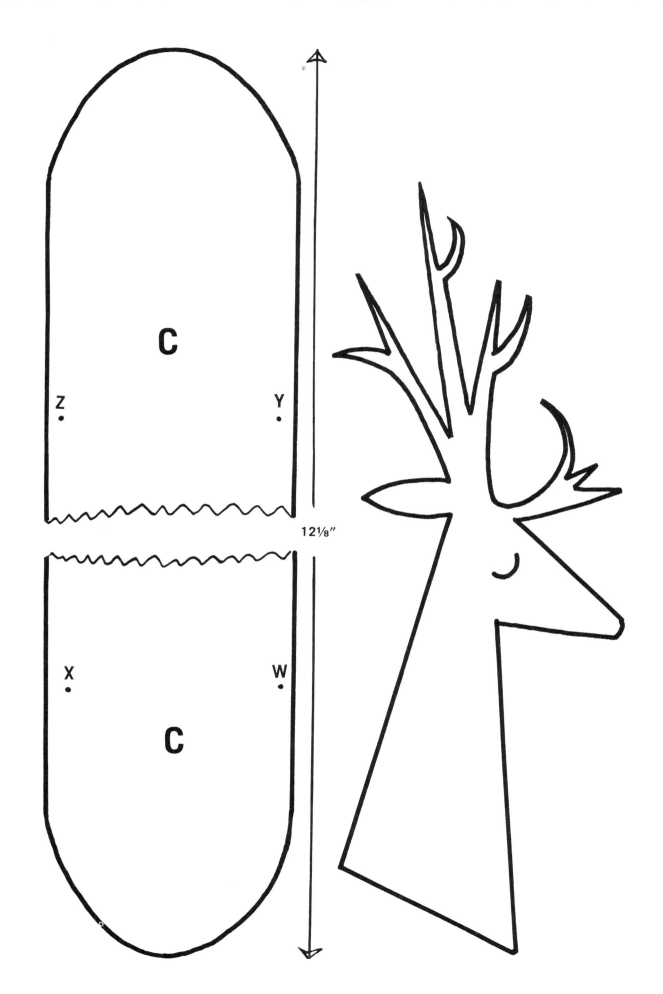

C

Z •

Y •

12 1/8"

X •

W •

C

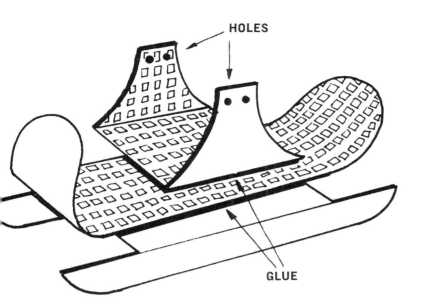

HOLES

GLUE

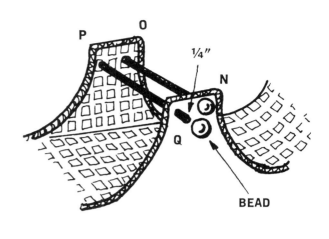

P   O

¼"

N

Q

BEAD

Slit and
glue.

PINE CONE

GLUE

LEGS

GLASS

(See color plate 9.) # CANDY DECORATED CHURCH

MATERIALS

2 slabs Styrofoam 12 x 26 x 2 inches
¼ inch plywood 24 x 62 inches
angle irons
short wood screws
foil and colored gift wrapping papers
cardboard
long bamboo skewers
straight pins
candies:
    jelly beans
    red hots
    mimosa balls
    gumdrops in various shapes and sizes

colored Chiclets
small silver cake balls
hard candies
soft mints
peppermint circles
chocolate sticks
chocolate drops covered with hard candy
licorice strings
strawberry rolls
candy corn
juju fruits
wintergreen disks
rubber cement
Sobo glue
plastic and masking tapes

Pattern　　1. Follow measurements on diagram and draw silhouette on *back* of Styrofoam slabs.

To cut out　　2. Use a saw to cut centers of church from one slab and wings from the other.

To join parts　　3. Lay pieces on flat surface and join with glue and skewers. Insert skewers into 2-inch edge of one piece. Keep them at right angles to edge. Coat adjoining edge with glue and press edges together. Be very careful that bottoms of both pieces are even. Allow to dry thoroughly.

4. Draw a line down center of front of church with a razor blade, *not* a pencil.

Pattern　　5. Lay church on brown paper and draw around it for silhouette of pattern. Draw a line down center of pattern. Draw in windows and door.

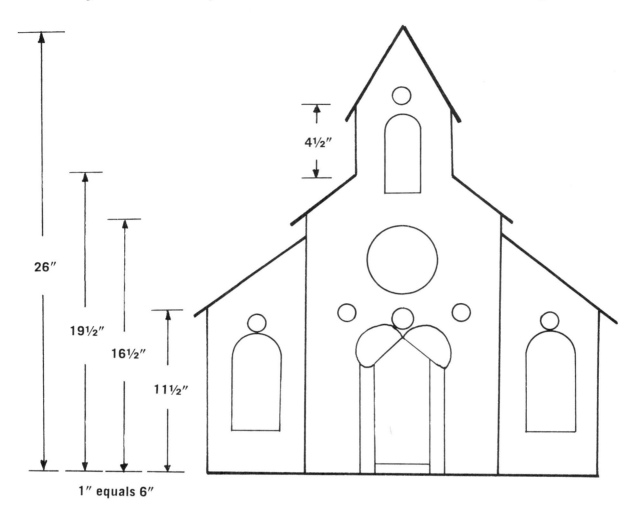

26″

19½″

16½″

11½″

4½″

1″ equals 6″

To attach candies

6. Arrange candies on pattern exactly as you will on church, to check proportions, colors, and positions. Use center line as guide and transfer candies to church with a pair of tweezers. A pair of dental tweezers with crook at end is ideal for this. Glue candies in place. Add straight pins to gum drops and soft mints to be sure they will stay in place. Use pins decoratively—in center of drops, at corners and center of flat pieces.

Allow 24 hours to dry. Keep work in cool, dry room. If working in a damp climate, an electric fan blowing on church constantly will keep candies from becoming sticky and runny.

7. Draw ½ inch inside of edge of church pattern to make pattern for the frame that will support the church. Cut this from plywood.

Frame

8. Cut base 12 x 30 inches from plywood, and draw line across center of length.

Base

9. Set frame 3 inches from and parallel to back edge of base. Join them with angle irons. If you are not a carpenter, get the help of a man or a skilled boy. File off points of screws that protrude through bottom of base.

To join base and frame

10. Lay frame flat on the edge of a table allowing base to overhang edge. Spread glue generously and evenly over frame. Spread glue on 2-inch base edge of church.

Lay church on glue-covered frame and press securely against frame and base. Be sure that center lines of church and base coincide. Dry for 24 hours.

To join church to base and frame

11. Cover edges of base with plastic tape and cement paper over top of base. Cut a slit, open at center back in paper to fit around and slightly under church.

To cover base

12. Arrange candies for steps, path, and flowerbeds on base. Glue in place.

Steps, path, flowerbeds

13. Cut 4-inch strips of cardboard for roof. Make each roof 3 inches longer than diagonal it will cover. Join parts of top roof with masking tape. Cement foil over and under roofs, leaving 1 inch width of cardboard exposed on center of underside. Punch hole in center of top roof's ridge. Glue roofs in place, holding with pins until dry.

Roof

14. Impale gumdrops on piece of skewer and insert through hole in ridge. Pin small gum drops along ridge.

(*See color plate 5.*) # PLACE CARDS

MATERIALS

old calling cards or 2- x 3-inch
   rectangles of 2-ply bristol board
felt-tipped marking pen

Day-Glo signal dots
pull tabs from soft-drink cans
Uhu glue

1. Practice making elongated S lines on scrap paper with the felt-tipped marker. When sufficiently skillful, draw one horizontal and one vertical S on card (see card in foreground of photograph 1).
2. Add C-shaped curls to lines as in photograph 1.
3. Apply signal dots, as in completed cards.
4. Write in name.
5. Flatten the tongue of a pull tab with a rolling pin.
6. Bend tongue upright, from *underside* of ring. Bend a bit further to place it at a slight slant back over the ring as in photograph 2.
7. Put drop of glue on end of tongue and press card in place.

VARIATIONS

Glue miniature shells, small feathers, tiny artificial or dried flowers, leaves, ferns, and grasses to cards as in photograph 2. Use small pearl beads and boutique trims for accents.

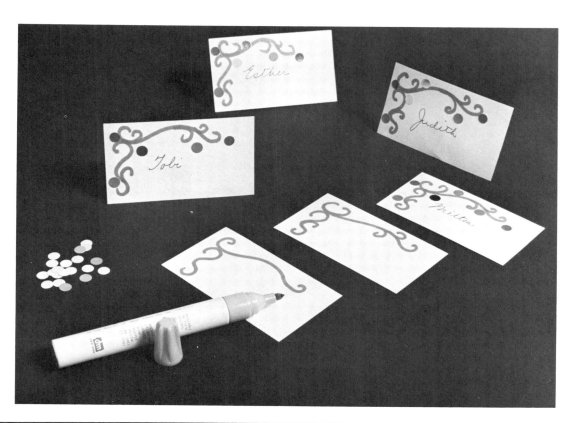

(See color plate 4.) # VALENTINE PARTY TABLE DECORATIONS

While designed primarily for children, these decorations are equally appropriate for an adult party. Just omit the shopping bag.

Use at least 3 shades of red for decorations: vermilion, magenta (shocking pink), and dark red. Use all of these colors on the flower-heart centerpiece. Repeat each color on one or more of the other items.

Use white dishes and serve pink, red, and white food, such as:

strawberry ice cream

vanilla ice cream and
  raspberry ice

vanilla ice cream, frozen straw-
  berries, and whipped cream

white cake with white icing
  (angel food and Martha
  Washington cake)

red or pink marzipan rolled between sheets of Saran wrap to ¼- or ⅛-inch thickness and hearts cut from it with cookie, sandwich, and aspic cutters. Decorate tops and sides of cake with these hearts. Or roll a thicker slab, cut out hearts, dry overnight, and serve as favors.

Allow each guest to take home his or her place card, place mat, drinking and nut cups, and napkin ring in the shopping bag with his name on it. When the guests are ready to leave, place the centerpiece on the hall table. Divide the number of flowers evenly among the number of guests. As he leaves, give each guest his share of the flowers.

To make patterns for hearts, fold a piece of brown wrapping paper lengthwise, draw a half heart on fold, and cut out (see diagram). Cut

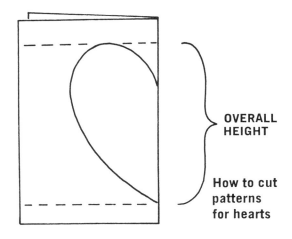

OVERALL HEIGHT

How to cut patterns for hearts

patterns for hearts with an overall height of 1½, 2½, 3, 4, and 5 inches for the items below unless other sizes are specified.

When a number of one color of the same size are needed, staple a stack of several sheets together and cut out a number of hearts at one time. Trace around pattern on back of paper for colored hearts. Fold white paper, draw half of heart pattern on fold, and cut out with pinking or scallop shears.

To dry-bond tissue to white paper, item 24, page 28.

Centerpiece of Flower-Hearts

MATERIALS

1-gallon white plastic bleach jug
styrene molded forms from
    packaging
brown wrapping paper
white paper
vermilion and magenta tissue
    paper
dark red flocked paper, velvet,
    or velveteen scraps

18-inch-long, gauge no. 21
    green-enameled florist wire
flat scrap metal, such as
    washers, hinges
butterfly ruffling
powdered white soap flakes
masking tape
rubber cement
Sobo and Uhu glues

1. Use scissors to cut 4-inch-deep bowl from bottom of jug.

2. To keep centerpiece from tipping, arrange flat scrap metal inside bottom of bowl and tape each piece down securely.

3. Cut disks from foam molds to fit inside bowl. Use Sobo to glue layers together and to scrap metal. Use Uhu to glue foam to sides of bowl.

4. Use Uhu to glue butterfly ruffling around top and bottom of bowl.

5. Dry-bond (see above) a sheet of vermilion and a sheet of magenta tissue to white paper.

6. Make approximately 6 large, 4 medium, and 24 small flower-hearts. Cut out 3-, 4-, and 5-inch-high white hearts and 2½-, 3-, and 4-inch-high colored hearts.

7. Cement colored hearts to center of one side of white hearts, as in photograph.

8. Use a fresh tube of Uhu glue. To cover the end of a piece of wire with glue, insert end into spout of tube. Glue covered end of wire on back (white side) of heart. Be careful that wire does not protrude beyond the colored heart on the other side.

9. When glue is dry, cement another colored heart over wire and in center of white heart.

10. When making large hearts with dark red, cover only one side of flower with it and the other with a tissue and white paper heart. The velvet, velveteen, and flocked paper are all heavy and can bend the wires on the tall, large flower-hearts if they are on both sides.

11. Grasp wire near lower end, push it carefully into foam; be sure that it goes through all the layers of foam to hold the flower steady.

12. Place the large flowers first, then the medium-sized ones, and the

smallest last. As you work, cut the wires progressively shorter, or curl them—first in one direction and then in the other—by pulling them between thumb and forefinger, to suggest the stems of live flowers.

13. When bowl is placed on the table, pour soap flakes over foam to cover soiled or uneven surfaces.

Place Mat

MATERIALS

2-ply bristol board	white paper
brown wrapping paper	rubber cement
magenta tissue paper	Uhu glue

1. Cut out 2 heart patterns, 18 wide x 14 inches high and 16 wide x 12½ inches high, respectively.

2. Cut from magenta and cement to large heart as in photograph.

3. Trace pattern for letters (page 95) and cut out of bristol board. Glue in place.

Place Card

MATERIALS

white paper	white poster paint or white ink
vermilion tissue paper	rubber cement
brown wrapping paper	Uhu glue
small, clear cylindrical plastic	
pill bottle	

1. Cut out 4-inch-high white heart and 3-inch-high vermilion heart. *Patterns*
2. Cement hearts together.

3. Write name with white ink; or with pencil, and go over the lines *Name*
with white paint.

4. Remove top from pill bottle and invert bottle. Glue heart to side *Stand*
of bottle.

Candlestick

MATERIALS

magenta plastic electric-
   typewriter ribbon spool
milky white spool from Scotch
   tape roll

butter doily
1½-inch steel washer
Uhu glue

Spools   1. Glue a ribbon spool to either end of a white spool.

Weight   2. Glue washer onto the underside of the lower typewriter spool.

Doily   3. Glue candlestick to doily. If butter doilies are not available, cut a 2¼-inch-wide circle with pinking or scallop shears.

CUP

Napkin Ring

MATERIALS

core from roll of plastic tape
  or toilet paper
ruffling

1-inch-wide decorative ribbon
  with heart motif
Uhu glue

Core   1. Cut core 1½ inches wide.

Ribbon   2. Glue ribbon around it.

Ruffling   3. Glue ruffling to edges.

Drinking Cup

MATERIALS

white plastic bleach bottle
magenta tissue paper
white paper

sandpaper
rubber cement
Uhu glue

Cup   1. Cut 4-inch-high cup from bottom of bottle. For small children leave edge flat; for older children cut curved edge as in photograph. Sand edge smooth.

Lettering   2. Dry-bond tissue and paper (see item 24, page 28). Trace pattern for lettering (page 95) and cut out of magenta. Glue in place.

Nut or Candy Cup

MATERIALS

white plastic top from spray can
brown wrapping paper
dark red flocked paper, velvet,
  or velveteen scraps

white paper
red foil
rubber cement
Uhu glue

Red sides   1. Cut strip of flocked paper or velvet the depth of plastic top. Cut top edge with pinking or scallop shears. Glue around top.

2. Cut 2½-inch-high white paper heart and 1⅛-inch-high foil heart.   *Hearts*
Cement hearts together.

3. Glue hearts to side of cup.

Shopping Bag

MATERIALS

small shopping bag 10 inches high	white paper
brown wrapping paper	magenta felt-tipped marking pen
magenta tissue paper	rubber cement

1. Cement dry-bonded tissue and white paper over bag.   *Cover of bag*

2. Cut out 5-inch-high heart and cement to side of bag as in photograph.   *Heart*

3. Use marking pen to write guest's name on bag.   *Name*

LIGHTED EGG TREE FOR EASTER

Use this as a table centerpiece or place it on the hall or living room table, mantel, or window sill. Light the tree at dusk. To show to best advantage, use subdued lighting in the rest of the room.

MATERIALS

white jumbo eggs
midget or miniature Christmas
   tree lights
bare branches with many twigs
rubber bands
1 pound cold cream jar or a vase

nuts, bolts, nails, screws,
   washers, etc.
small stones
invisible mending tape
Sobo glue
eye dropper

To collect eggs   1. Depending on the size and egg-eating capacity of your family, begin blowing eggs days or even weeks before making the tree. Scrambled eggs and omelettes are the obvious dishes to serve while collecting shells, but any recipe that uses whole, unseparated eggs will be a pleasant change in this menu.

Choice of lights   2. Jumbo eggs are large enough to hold midget lights, which will make a more brilliantly lighted tree. Smaller eggs usually can accommodate miniature lights, which are not as bright.

The lights used here are a string of 35 midget lights. A number of shorter strings can be substituted for this. On a larger tree, several long strings of 35 or 50 can be used; more short strings are equally suitable.

To blow eggs   3. Use a needle or push pin to punch holes in each egg. Make a $\frac{1}{4}$ inch circle of holes in the center of the large end and a single, slightly enlarged hole in the narrow end. Remove circles of shell and membrane

formed by circle of holes. Pierce inner membrane that encloses albumen and enlarge hole to the size of the hole in the shell.

Hold egg over bowl and blow through small hole to empty shell. Wash out inside. Wash off outside with dishwater detergent to remove grease and stains. Rinse well and drain.

To coat inside with glue

4. To make egg shell stronger, make a solution of 2 parts glue to 1 part water and pour ½ teaspoon of it into the egg with an eye dropper. Hold finger over holes and shake solution in egg until entire interior is coated. Pour out excess, drain and allow egg to dry thoroughly. Store shells in egg cartons in a safe place until ready to use.

To enlarge hole

5. Use manicure or embroidery scissors to snip off bits of shell and enlarge the big hole of each egg. Test a hole's size with a light to find how much space is needed to insert light.

To join shells to lights

6. Insert light and close opening with criss-crossed strips of tape around the protruding cord. Do not be stingy with tape, but keep ends around the mouth of the hole. At most, no strip of tape should extend more than a quarter of the way up the shell's side, preferably less.

Tree

7. Make an attractive arrangement of the branches. To keep the arrangement's shape, wrap the bottom of the stems with rubber bands.

Stand

8. Place the tree in the jar or vase. Pour the nuts, bolts, etc. around it. Be careful to keep the tree upright; keep the bottom of the branches touching the bottom of the jar. Fill the jar almost full and then cover the hardware with stones.

To arrange the lights

9. Begin with the middle of the string of lights and start draping them over the top of the tree. If possible, have some one help you, as the tree will be top heavy at first. Gradually work down on the tree on each side, working back and forth toward the center. Hang eggs between branches as well as on them. The wires and twigs will be indistinguishable at a short distance.

If you use more than one string of lights, tape an extension cord with a multiple socket to the back of the container. Then the lights can be plugged into it and only a single cord will lead away from the tree.

ALTERNATE

Using lights on a Christmas tree follows.

Lighted Eggs for Christmas Tree   *(See color plate 2.)*

Make strings of lighted eggs as described above. The tree can be lighted solely with these or they can be used in addition to miniature lights. Place the miniature lights close to the trunk and on the center of the branches. After they have been arranged, add the egg lights to the outer ends of the branches.

Begin at the top of the tree with the center of the string, as on the Egg Tree. Hang tinsel garlands after the lights are in place. If desired, ornaments can then be hung on the tree.

GIANT EASTER EGG

MATERIALS

balloon
rubber band
tissue paper, white and several
  shades of green
spray starch
white poster paint

Wright's tape and butterfly
  ruffling
artificial flowers and leaves
blown or hard-boiled eggs
food coloring
Uhu glue
upholstery needle
push pin

1. Blow up balloon, twist, and tie neck into knot. Check size of balloon to see if it can be set on a trivet and both can fit in the oven. Wrap rubber band around neck of balloon, below knot.

Papier maché

2. Cut 60 sheets of white tissue paper into 2½-inch-wide strips.

3. Work over the sink. Spray balloon with starch and crisscross with strips of tissue. Respray and apply more strips. Continue to spray and add tissue, being sure to crisscross strips and to cover balloon evenly. Handle gently and if tissue becomes soggy, add enough strips to absorb moisture before spraying again.

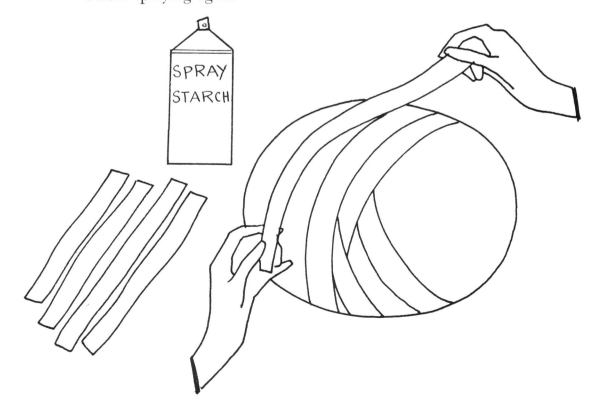

4. Light oven and turn it to *lowest* possible heat. Place balloon on trivet in oven and *leave door open*. Turn balloon slightly every 5 minutes so that it will not stick to the trivet.

Drying

If heat is too high, balloon may expand enough to burst tissue. If this happens, remove from oven, cool slightly, and repair tear with more starch and crisscrossed tissue strips. Keep repair loose, for air inside will expand again. Replace balloon-egg in oven and lower heat.

After 30 minutes, turn egg only occasionally. Allow 2 or 3 hours or more to dry. Pierce egg in half-dozen places with heavy darning or upholstery needle.

Paint   5. Stir paint well and apply undiluted to the egg. Replace in oven and dry again.

Ruffling   6. Tie a string around center of egg and draw along it with a pencil. Glue taped ruffling along this line. Fold butterfly ruffling in half by doubling over, so that ruffled edges are together, and iron flat. Glue 3 lines of this doubled ruffling above and 3 below taped ruffling. Use yellow-edged butterfly ruffling for the middle line each time.

Flowers   7. Arrange artificial flowers as in photograph and glue in place. Cut additional leaves from several shades of green tissue. Fold down center, open, and glue bottom tips to egg.

Painted eggs   8. Paint blown or hard-boiled eggs with food coloring. Vary intensity of shades on eggs and leave a few white.
          To blow eggs, use a needle or push pin to punch holes. Make a small $\frac{1}{8}$-inch-wide circle of holes in the center of the large end and a single, slightly enlarged hole in the center of the narrow end. Remove circles of shell and membrane formed by holes in the large end. Hold over bowl and blow through single hole to empty egg. Save contents for scrambled eggs. Wash out inside of egg and wash off outside with dishwasher detergent to remove grease. Rinse well, drain, and dry. Paint.

Nest   9. Use several shades of green tissue and cut each sheet into 1-inch-wide strips. Toss until shades are thoroughly mixed. Form into nest.
          10. Set large egg in center and surround with colored eggs.

ANGEL AND LAMB MOBILE

MATERIALS

foil gift-wrapping paper
felt-tipped marking pens
thread
needle

green-enameled florist wire
rubber cement
push pin

1. Cement 2 pieces of foil paper back to back. Trace patterns from page 107. Trace onto foil with blunt pencil. Cut out figure.

*To trace
and cut out*

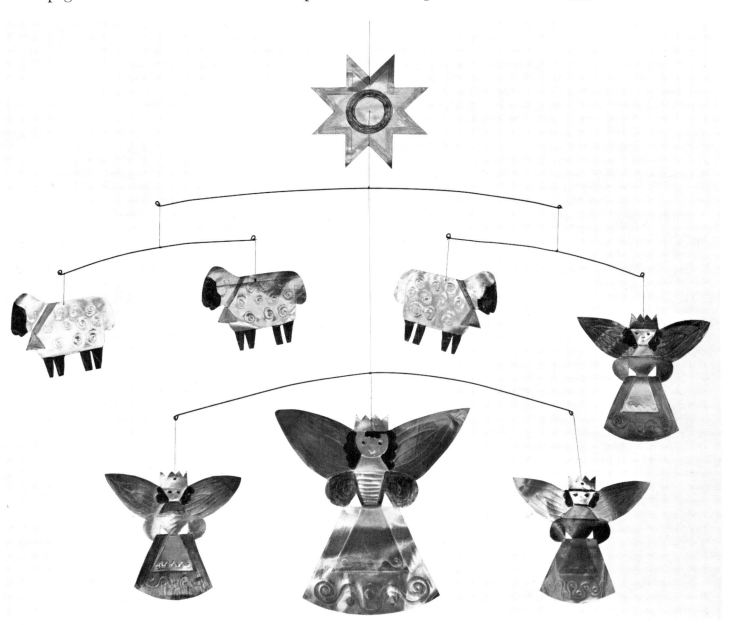

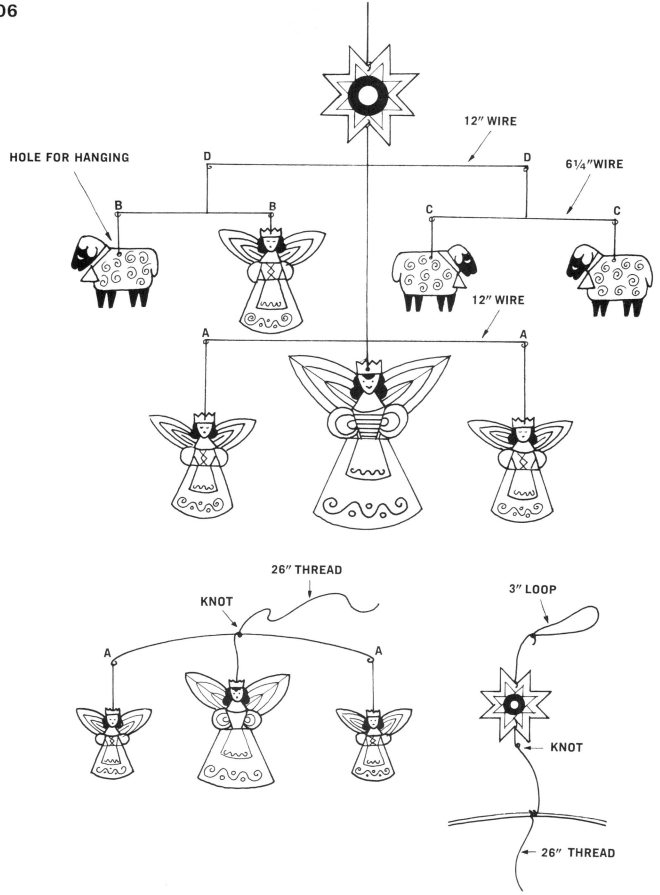

HOLE FOR HANGING

12" WIRE

6¼" WIRE

D   D

B   B

C   C

12" WIRE

A   A

26" THREAD

KNOT

A   A

3" LOOP

KNOT

26" THREAD

2. Use marking pens to color figures and to draw in details. Allow *To color* to dry thoroughly, then color other side of figures.

3. Cut 4 pieces of wire 12, 6¼, 6¼, and 12 inches long. Use long *Wire* nose pliers to make tiny closed loops at both ends of each wire. Curve wires slightly by gently pulling the complete length through fingers. Do this with one continuous pull. Do not bend a bit at a time.

To assemble threading   4. With a needle, punch a hole in top of each figure where shown on pattern. Thread needle, knot thread, and run through hole. Allow a good length of thread to tie to wire. Prepare all figures in this manner.

Hanging   5. Hang and balance angels on lower wire first. When tying thread to wire, wind it around the wire several times before knotting and cutting off end.

Lower wire   6. Hang large angel on 26-inch thread. Knot angel several times to center of wire. Do *not* cut thread. Gently push knot back and forth along wire until angels on end are balanced when you hold wire by long thread from center angel.

Center wires   7. Tie lambs and angel to center wires as you did angels to lower wire. Tie thread with several knots to center of each wire. Push knots back and forth until each is balanced on thread. Tie threads to ends of top wire.

To join wires   8. Bring up thread from the large angel and tie it to the center of the top wire. Push knots back and forth until all figures are balanced.

9. Thread needle with end of 26-inch center thread. Make a knot under the star. Stitch in and out of star. Knot end of thread in a 3-inch loop for hanging.

EASTER ANGEL CAROUSEL

MATERIALS

patterned and foil gift-wrapping paper	button or carpet thread
yellow tissue paper	straight pins
Styrofoam cone 6½ inches high, 2⅞ inches across base	felt-tipped marking pen
	tiny gold beads
10-inch-long thin knitting needle	staples
	rubber cement
1- and 3-ply bristol board	Uhu glue

Canopy

1. Follow diagram page 110 and draw 3 concentric circles with radii 5⅝, 4⅜, and 1¾ inches on 3-ply board. Divide disk in sixteenths. Cut out disk and cut away C.

To cut out

Connect points a, b, c, and d with straight lines. Cut lines ab, bc, and cd with single-edged razor blade. Score line ad. Roll disk into cone and fold out rectangles. Then press cone and rectangles flat again. Punch holes at all 3 f and g points.

To cover underside

2. Cement paper to underside of disk. Cut 1-inch strip beyond A for overlapping. Leave flap and A uncemented. Cut rectangle flaps in paper through slits in board.

To cover top

3. Draw a circle with a 6⅛-inch radius on patterned paper. Use scallop or pinking shears to cut out. Follow instruction 2 and cement in place over top of canopy, leave overlap and A uncemented, and cut slits.

4. Form canopy by overlapping A and B. Staple and glue board together. Cement paper A's and flaps down.

Stand

5. Push knitting needle through the center of base up through tip of Styrofoam cone until needle's head is flush with cone's base.

To cover stand

6. Cut semicircle of 6 layers of tissue. Roll around cone and pin in place. Trim bottom even.

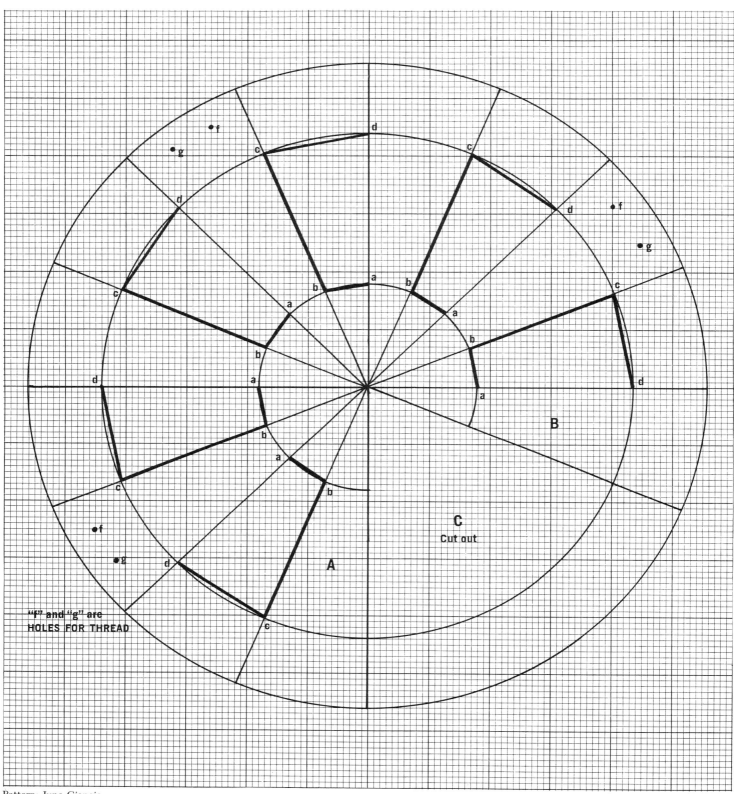

Pattern: June Ciancio

Angels   7. Cement foil paper on either side of 1-ply board. Trace pattern, page 111, onto foil and cut out. Use scallop or pinking shears to cut them. Color exposed edge of board with marking pen. Punch holes at f and g. Use a blunt pencil to draw details of costume, eyes, and hair on both sides of angel.

To attach angels   8. Match holes f and g on angel and canopy. Knot thread and run *to canopy* through back of angel at f, under canopy and out at f, across and into g, down and into g on front of angel. Knot at back, being sure that all 3 angels hang at equal distance from canopy's edge.

To balance canopy   9. Place canopy on point of needle. Where canopy tips highest, glue small beads, one at a time, to underside. Fold out flaps at even distances, as in photograph.

To turn   10. To turn carousel, place it on a hot radiator, before a small fan or in a draft.

ALTERNATE

Cut canopy and angels from aluminum cans or tin cans. Color with marking pens. Make a metal cone for stand. Set birthday candles under outer edges of canopy to turn it.

Use canopy and stand to suspend other figures appropriate for particular events.

Children's Party Ideas for Fourth of July, Halloween, and Birthdays

114

GLORIOUS-FOURTH PARADE BAND

Form a parade of children of various ages with these instruments. Tiny and small children can bang the pans and shake the rattles. Older children can carry the tune on the comb, big jug, and megaphone. The oldest can beat fairly complicated rhythms on the drum and washboard, adding accents with the jingle bells and triangle. Hold a brief rehearsal before the parade begins.

OPTIONAL ADDITIONS

A flag-bearer can head the parade. A drum major or majorette can lead the band. For his baton, attach a large tassel or pompon (see item 27, page 29) to the top of a broomstick with a push pin. Wrap red, white, and blue ribbons in a spiral around the broomstick. An old tassel from clothes, cushion, or drapery can be used.

GENERAL SUGGESTIONS

Braid a band from 6 strands of wool or use a ready-made dressmaker's braided band from which to hang the drum.

Dismantle a 3-armed metal towel rack. Use the arms to tap the triangle, metal soap dish, or any other scrap-metal instrument. The rectangle that holds the arms and was attached to the wall can be screwed to the top of the stick rattle.

If these particular pieces of scrap metal are not available or if you want more instruments, hang assorted metal objects on loops of string and tap with a knife to find which will give the best sounds.

Soap Dish

MATERIALS

cut-work metal soap dish
¾-inch-wide red, white, and
   blue braid
gold medallion

staples
Sobo glue
towel-rack rod (see general
   suggestions above)

1. Suspend soap dish on a 2-foot length of braid. Hold ends together ***To hang*** and fold over to form a 6-inch loop at top. Staple at 2 inches below top of loop and glue medallion over staple as in photograph.

2. Tap and bang soap dish with towel rack or other metal object. ***To play***

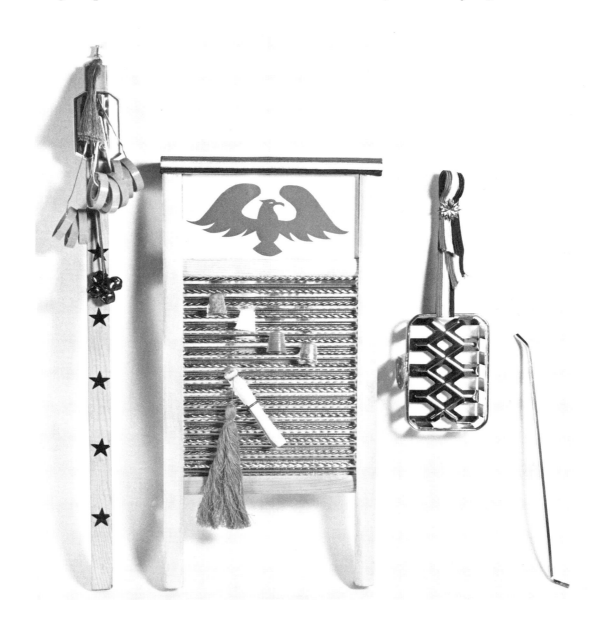

Stick Rattle

MATERIALS

22-inch-length of ⅞-inch-
   wide lath
sandpaper
towel-rack holder (see general
   suggestions above)
wood screws
plastic spools from electric-
   typewriter ribbon

gold, red, and blue soutache
   braids
sleigh bells
gum-backed stars
tassel
push pin
Uhu glue

Lath　　1. Sand until smooth.

Rack holder　　2. Attach rack holder to lath with screws 1 inch from top.

Plastic spools　　3. Hang 3 plastic spools on a loop of soutache braid from each of the 3 cylinders that hold rods. Knot braid and pull knots inside cylinders.

Sleigh bells　　4. On a longer loop hang 5 sleigh bells from the lowest cylinder.

Stars　　5. Glue 6 stars to lath as in photograph.

Tassel　　6. Attach tassel (see item 27, page 29) to top of lath with push pin. Be sure that pin is pushed in all the way.

To play　　7. Shake stick.

Washboard

MATERIALS

washboard
clothespin
thimbles:
   metal
   plastic: red, white, blue
thread

tassel
paper or Con-Tact
dressmaker's braid
Uhu and Sobo glue
¾-inch braid

1. Use any size washboard. This one is small, 8½ x 18 inches, which is easy for a little child to carry and play. **Size**

2. Cover the top panel with white paper or Con-Tact. Trace the pattern above of the eagle and cut out of dark blue paper or Con-Tact. Attach to panel with glue if paper, with pressure if Con-Tact. **Decorations**

Use Sobo to glue ¾-inch red, white, and blue braid around top edge.

3. Tie tassel (see page 29, item 27) to one end of a length of thread; tie other end around clothespin, just under head. Make thread long enough for tassel to dangle freely when clothespin is rubbed on board. **Clothespin**

4. Hold the board horizontally on the left arm, its legs against the player's body. A small child can happily rub the clothespin head back and forth along the ridges of the washboard. **To play**

An older child can wear 3 or 4 thimbles on his right hand and with them rub, drum, or tap with the thimbles' tips and sides on the ridges. By combining these techniques, he can produce a variety of sounds.

Triangle

MATERIALS

copper rod from filing cabinet drawer	stainless-steel table knife or towel-rack rod
red middy braid	Sobo glue
¾-inch-wide red, white, and blue braid	staples

Triangle   1. Bend copper rod into triangle. Use 2 pairs of pliers.

To hang   2. Hang from loosely tied middy braid. Do not make knot tight against rod or the sound will be muffled. Staple ends of braid together.

Bow   3. Glue bow of wide braid to ends of middy braid.

To play   4. Tap sides or insides with knife or rod.

Tin Pie Pans

MATERIALS

tin pie pans
paper: red, white, blue
gum-backed stars

gold notarial seal
Uhu glue

1. Use scallop shears to cut out paper circles to fit inside bottom of pans. Use Uhu to glue one in the bottom of each pan.

Cut out paper stars (see item 16, page 26) 5, 3½, and 2 inches wide. Place on top of one another as in photograph. Glue together and then in center of circle in each pan.

Glue gum-backed stars between points of largest stars.

Inside decorations

2. Cut out 5-inch-wide stars and glue to back of pans. Use Uhu to glue gum-backed stars to pan and notarial seal to centers of large stars as in photograph.

Outside decorations

3. Strike edges of pans against one another. Vary rhythm and sound by banging backs of pans together.

To play

Cymbals

MATERIALS

2 pan tops or 2 pie pans and
2 hand-lotion bottle caps
red, white, and blue dressmaker's
braid

Uhu glue

1. If pie pans are used, glue a bottle cap in the center of the back of each and allow to dry overnight.

Pans

2. Glue braid around edges of cymbals as in photograph. For a less muffled sound, omit braid. Instead, tie tassels to handles.

Braid

3. Hold by handles and bang cymbals together, either directly against each other or with a slightly sliding motion.

To play

Foil Pie Pans

MATERIALS

colored foil pie pans (frozen   Venice-lace daisies
cakes are sold in them)   Uhu glue

Decorations   1. Glue circle of daisies to outside of one pan. Leave other undecorated for better sound.

To play   2. Scrape rims across each other and tap against each other.
A single undecorated pan can be tapped with knuckles or beaten lightly with fist. For a different sound, a single decorated pan can be beaten lightly with a cork-tipped drum stick (see drum, below).

Jingle Bells

MATERIALS

wire coathangers or rod from   tissue paper
filing drawer   brass rings or house numbers
white rags   nylon fishing line
red and blue ribbons   plastic tape
cylindrical and large faceted   Sobo and Uhu glue
beads
core from roll of cash-register
or adding-machine paper or core
from package handle

Coathanger   1. Follow diagram opposite to bend coathanger into Y shape. Break off hook.

Horizontal rod   2. Cut a 12½-inch section of straight wire from a second coathanger or from a rod. Insert through loops of coathanger as in diagram.

Padding   3. Cut strips of white rags and wrap around V of Y. Use Sobo to glue ends in place. Spiral with ribbons and glue them in place.

Beads   4. Use Uhu to glue beads to end of horizontal rod.

5. Follow diagram to wrap wire with strips of tissue paper. Dab tissue with either glue and insert into roll's core. If package handle is used, tissue can be omitted.

Handle

6. Hang 2 brass rings or house numbers from a loop of nylon line. Tie 2 of these (4 rings on 2 loops) to center of rod. Follow manufacturer's instructions for knotting nylon. Hold line in place on rod with plastic tape.

Jingles

7. Shake gently.

To play

Round Rattle

MATERIALS

foil pie pans	tassel
large, hollow plastic beads or	staples
dried beans and peas	Uhu glue
dressmaker's fancy braid	

1. Place 6 beads (be sure they are very lightweight) or a handful of beans and peas between 2 pans. Staple edges together in 3 or 4 places.

To assemble and join parts

2. Staple braid around edges and a tassel that hangs freely. Crisscross strips of braid in center of pan and glue in place.

Decorations

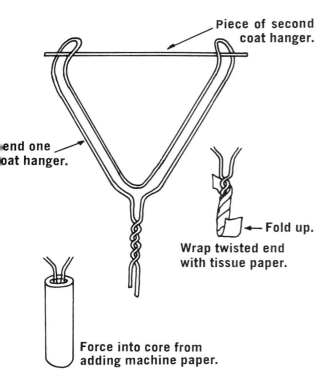

Piece of second coat hanger.

end one oat hanger.

Fold up.

Wrap twisted end with tissue paper.

Force into core from adding machine paper.

To play   3. Shake vigorously, or for a maraca effect, hold horizontally and move with short, single jerks—so that the beads all jump and land simultaneously.

Comb

MATERIALS

red or blue comb   white tissue paper

Comb and paper   1. Fold a piece of tissue paper over comb, with points of comb lying in fold. Cut extra pieces of tissue paper for child to carry in his pocket, as paper may become damp with playing and may need to be replaced.

To play   2. Hum, with mouth open and lips resting gently against the tissue paper.

Drum

MATERIALS

round metal cookie box   sandpaper
white Con-Tact   knitting-needle cork balls
gold braid   masking tape
wool yarn or braided strap   Uhu glue
3/8-inch dowel rods

Drum head   1. Cover each side of cookie box with 2 layers of Con-Tact for a "real drum" sound.

Decorations   2. Glue gold braid around edges of drum head with Uhu.

Neck strap   3. With an ice pick or awl, punch a hole in the center of side and enlarge with a bottle opener. Braid yarn or cut a yard of strap (see general suggestions above), and insert both ends in hole. Knot ends together firmly and attach knot to inside of box with tape and glue. Replace top.

4. Cut 2 10½-inch lengths of dowel and sand. Insert ends into corks.   ***Drum sticks***

5. Hang drum around neck, or tie around waist. Beat with drum sticks.   ***To play***

Jug and Bottle

MATERIALS

white plastic bleach bottle	gum-backed stars
white plastic bleach jug	Uhu glue
red and blue plastic tapes	

1. Remove labels from jug and bottle. Wash thoroughly and be sure all bleach is completely washed from the inside. Allow to drain and dry.   ***To clean jug and bottle***

Stripes   2. Decorate with stripes of plastic.

Stars   3. Use Uhu to glue on stars.

To play   4. Play jug by blowing a Bronx cheer across the top of the mouth of the jug and humming simultaneously.

Play bottle by blowing slightly down as well as across the opening to produce a foghorn sound.

The tone can be varied on both jug and bottle by filling them partially with water. Increase and decrease the water to raise and lower the tones.

Megaphone

MATERIALS

cone-shaped wax container (this
   held papaya juice) or a cone made
   of 2-ply bristol board
red, white, and blue decorated
   paper or Con-Tact

package handle
red or blue plastic tape
Uhu glue

Cone   1. If cone-shaped carton is not available, roll a long narrow cone of bristol board (see item 18, page 27). Make this from a semicircle, cut from 2 concentric circles. The inner circle should be small, for the mouth of the megaphone.

Cover   2. Glue decorated paper over cone or cover it with Con-Tact.

Handle   3. Cover handle with Con-Tact as in photograph. Twist copper ends of handle in opposite directions so that each copper loop will lie flat against cone. Place on seam where paper or Con-Tact overlaps. Attach loops with squares of tape. Slit each square where wrinkles form beside the loops. Overlap the edges of the slits.

To play   4. Sing or hum tune through the megaphone. Call out marching directions with it for the band.

PAPER BAG MASKS

(See color plate 1.)

The masks can be used for "Trick or Treat" or with either of the pantomimes which follow the directions. A pantomime can be the star event of a party for children. *Willy, the Wise Old Owl* is for 5- to 8-year-olds, *Intergalaxy Pantomime* for 9 to 12. Their subjects do not limit them to Halloween; they can be used at parties for various occasions, including birthdays.

The masks can be stored for a repeat performance or can be given to the guests. If there are more than eight or nine guests, be sure to have duplicates for those children who have been in the audience. For a party of actors only, parents and neighbors can be invited to attend the production.

The pantomimes have been used successfully in schools; *Willy the Wise Old Owl* with first- and second-graders. In one of its productions, for reasons peculiar to the situation, there were two princesses. This was a great success and was repeated at a request performance for the school's kindergarten class. Battle for the Cosmic Universe was equally successful with fourth-, fifth-, and sixth-graders.

You can introduce other variations in plot and cast in either pantomime as occasion requires, such as extra slaves, goblins, cohorts, and servants for larger casts. Use your imagination and experiment freely. Lots of action, particularly running and chasing, are always popular.

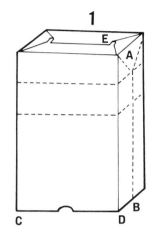

MATERIALS

heavy brown paper bags	masking tape
11 x 18 x 6¾ inches	invisible mending tape
gift-wrapping yarn	notarial seals
gift-wrapping ribbon	tracing or shelf paper
gift-wrapping paper or Con-Tact	rubber cement
felt-tipped marking pens	Uhu glue
staples	American flag

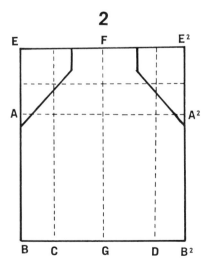

1. Open bag along bottom, gently prying glued areas loose, and flatten bag along center of sides, seams AB, diagram 1. Extend these to make seams EAB and $E^2A^2B^2$.

To prepare bags

To fold bags   2. Fold bag along center on line FG; press flat with back of knife to make a sharp fold. Reverse fold on back (seamed side) of bag to form convex fold. The fold FG on front will be your guide for centering face and features.

To trim corners   3. Cut off corners B and B² diagonally to fit over child's shoulders.
for shoulders   Round edges where patterns indicate.

Patterns   4. Trace pattern and enlarge by squares (see page 24, item 12).

Eyes on bag   5. Trace outline of eyes on front (unseamed side) of bag. Cut out eyes, making them ⅛ inch larger all around than on the pattern. Put 2 strips of mending tape between eyes on both front and inside of bag. This is important, for if this area is not reinforced, it may tear. If necessary, cut off tape that overlaps eye openings.

To outline   6. Trace outline of pattern on bag and cut out outline at the top.
pattern and   Use the outline of diagram 2 for the King, Servant, and Princess. Cut a
to shape top   different outline for each of the other masks as indicated on patterns.
              Glue and staple top edges of each mask together. Fold masking tape over the seam.

To cover   7. Cement paper or Con-Tact over bag. Line inside bottom edge with a 6-inch-wide strip to match outside.

Faces   8. Trace silhouette of face or features on front of mask; use fold FG to center pattern.
              9. Where face is a separate color from background, such as King, Servant, Princess, and Wizard, cut out face. Trace features on it and assemble complete face, minus yarns and ribbons. Draw in features of King, Servant, and Princess with marking pens.
              10. Cut out eyes *very* carefully. Put another 2 strips of mending tape between them on the back of the face. Trim off excess tape that overlaps openings. Draw around edges of eyes with marking pen.
              11. Center face on fold FG. Be sure eyes are over openings in background; cement face in place.
              12. On Wizard, reinforce back of horns with stiff paper.

To dry   13. Resist the temptation at this time to try on mask. Allow at least 2 or 3 hours, preferably 12, for the fumes of the cement to dissipate.

14. Princess: Glue yarn hair in place, as in photograph, one strand at a time. Trim evenly across top and glue one strand horizontally along top edge to support the bottom line of ribbon on the crown.

King: Cut lengths of glossy, gift-wrapping ribbon. Curl over knife blade. Glue 2 rows, overlapped, along top edge of mask below crown. Make moustache and beard of ribbon.

Servant: Follow directions for King. Omit dome of crown (see below) to make flat, pillbox hat. Omit beard and make hair and moustache light brown.

Hair

15. Cut out crowns; glue over rectangles at top of masks. Decorate with ribbons and cut-outs of paper and Con-Tact.

Crowns

16. Make one Goblin or the Slave of red paper and the other Goblin or Cohort X of green paper. Glue on dominos (on green paper, make the domino orange), then yarn hair and yarn moustache. For nose, fold square of paper diagonally into 4 sections (see diagrams 3 and 4). Glue the outside quarters down. Leave center quarters projecting to cover top of moustache.

Goblin, Slave, and Cohort X

17. Cover bag with pink-and-white striped paper. Make domino blue, nose bright red. Omit moustache. Make touseled hair of various colored yarns for the Monster Lady and of strips of aluminum foil or of tinsel ribbon for the Abominable Moll.

Monster Lady or Abominable Moll

18. Trace pattern and cut out parts. Cement in place, being careful that eyes and center folds overlap.

Owl

19. Reinforce helmet beyond edge of bag with heavy paper. Make helmet white. Make the glass over the face of foil, with red for the upper edge and blue the lower. Make the rectangle below of red. Glue an American flag in the rectangle above the glass.

Astronaut

20. Children must *not* carry lighted candles, lanterns, or pumpkins while wearing masks. Do *not* burn candles at parties where children are wearing paper masks.

Safety precautions

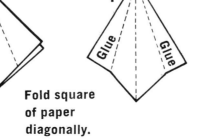

3 **4**

Fold square of paper diagonally.

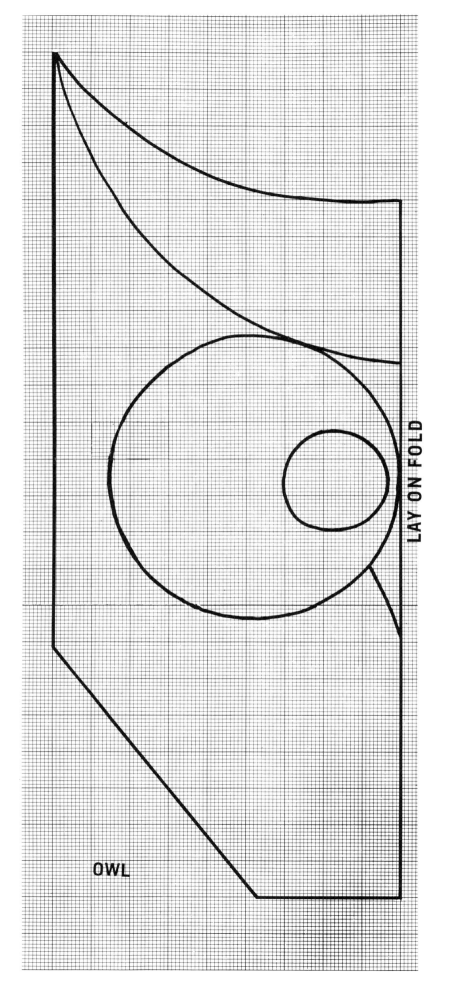

OWL

LAY ON FOLD

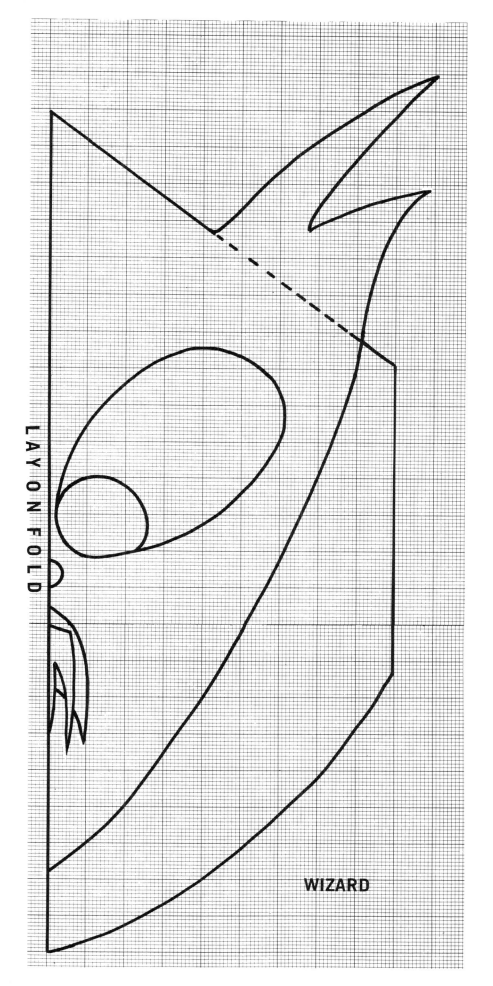

LAY ON FOLD

WIZARD

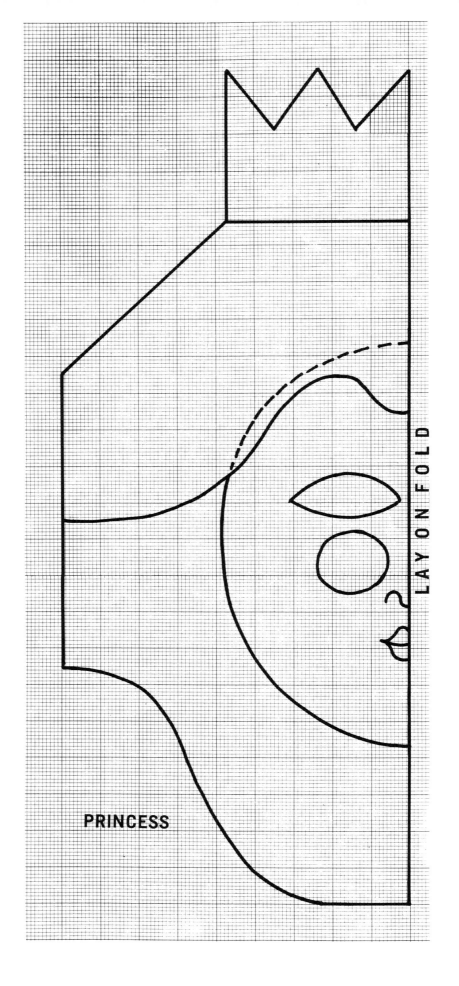

LAY ON FOLD

PRINCESS

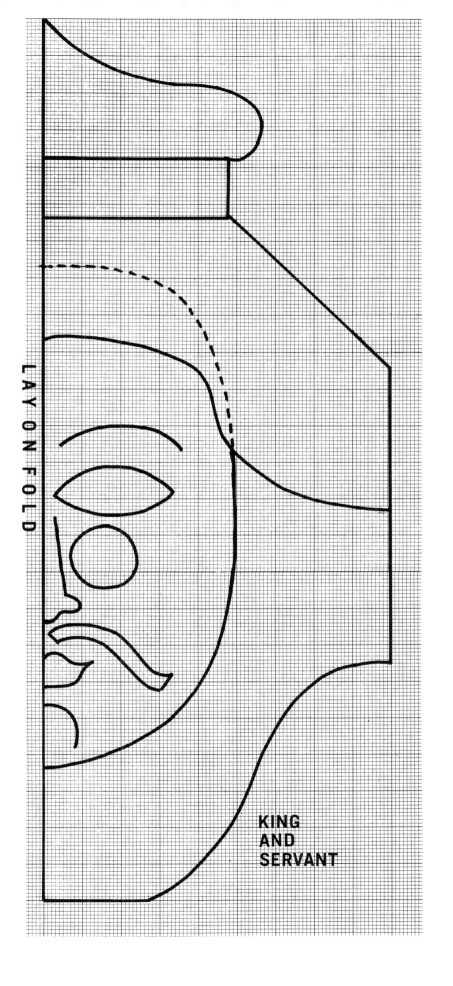

LAY ON FOLD

KING
AND
SERVANT

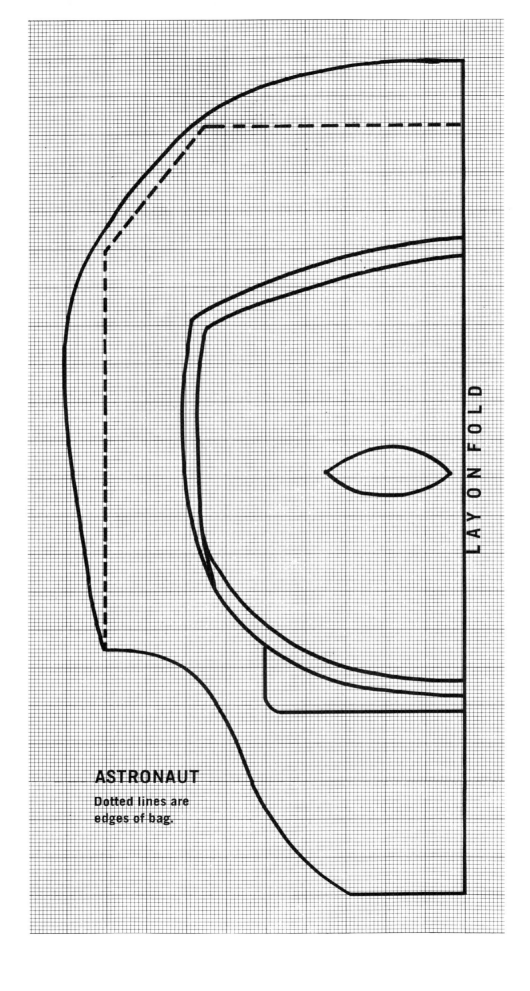

LAY ON FOLD

ASTRONAUT

Dotted lines are
edges of bag.

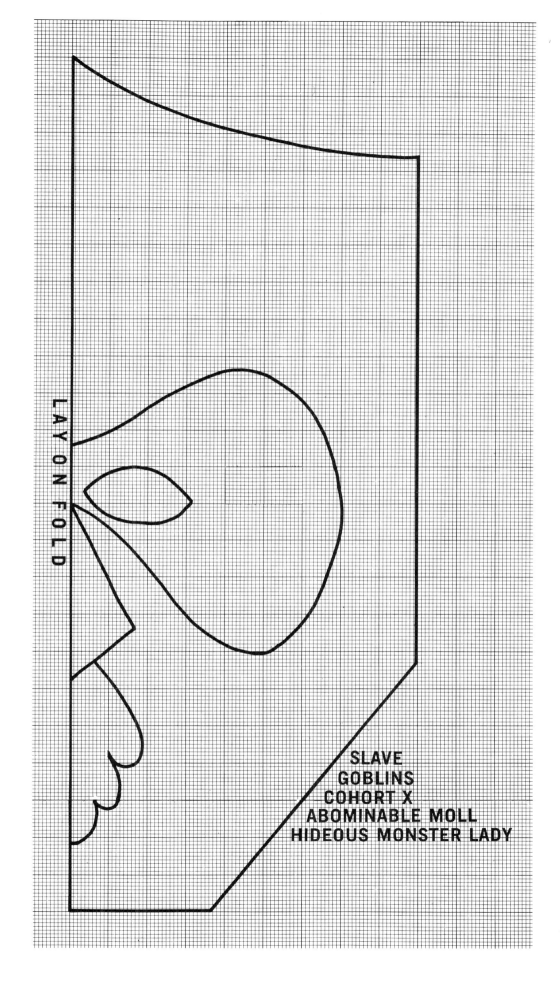

LAY ON FOLD

SLAVE
GOBLINS
COHORT X
ABOMINABLE MOLL
HIDEOUS MONSTER LADY

WILLY THE WISE OLD OWL

A PANTOMIME WITH MASKS

Stuart R. McLeod
Elizabeth D. Logan

Directions to the narrator: Read the scenario aloud to the guests before assigning roles. Specify particular areas in the room for each locale. The Tower and its four doors should be four chairs placed in a circle. The Princess, Wizard, and Goblins are each assigned a particular chair in which to sit when he is not performing. Other areas will be the Garden of the Princess and the Castle of the King with a garden beside it.

Once the guests have listened to the story, the roles are assigned, masks put on, and the narrator reads the scenario again, allowing the actors time to perform each action by appropriate gestures, movements, and sound effects (no other props are needed).

CAST OF CHARACTERS IN ORDER OF APPEARANCE

PRINCESS	KING
WIZARD	KING'S SERVANT
TWO GOBLINS	HIDEOUS MONSTER LADY
WILLY THE OWL	

Once there was a beautiful Princess who was gathering flowers in her garden.

Suddenly a wicked Wizard leaped over the wall and tried to pull her away.

The Princess screamed and tried to get away from the Wizard.

But he was a very strong Wizard and he finally carried her away with him to his Fantastic Tower.

He told her he would keep her a prisoner until she promised to marry him.

The Princess shook her head and refused.

The Wizard stamped his foot angrily and went away.

(continued after color insert)

Paper Bag Masks, page 125. PHOTOGRAPH: Al Tosca. Reprinted by permission from the October, 1971, issue of *Good Housekeeping Magazine,* © 1971 by the Hearst Corporation

PLATE 1

Felt Wall Hanging, page 217. Reprinted from *Better Homes and Gardens Christmas Ideas*

Spool Christmas Tree Ornaments, page 51
PHOTOGRAPH: the author

Lighted Eggs for the Christmas Tree, page 98
PHOTOGRAPH: the author

PLATE 2

Christmas Tree Ornaments, page 48
PHOTOGRAPH: the author

Paper and Cardboard Creche, page 67. Reprinted from
Better Homes and Gardens Christmas Ideas

PLATE 3

Valentine Party Table Decorations, page 90
Table Setting. PHOTOGRAPH: the author

Centerpiece: PHOTOGRAPH: the author

Bag and Souvenirs. PHOTOGRAPH: the author

PLATE 4

Place Cards and Pull Tab Stand, page 88
PHOTOGRAPH: the author

Stone Figures, page 186. PHOTOGRAPH: the author

Stone Faces, page 186. PHOTOGRAPH: the author

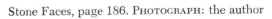

PLATE 5

Medieval Spool Village, page 204. PHOTOGRAPH: Richard Bianchi. Copyright 1966 *McCall's Magazine*. Reprinted with permission

PLATE 6

Glorious Fourth Parade Band, **pages 120-124**

TOP. Foil Pie Pan, Combs, Round Rattle and Jingle Bells

BOTTOM. Megaphone, Drum, Jug and Bottle

ALL PHOTOGRAPHS: the author

PLATE **7**

Tin Can Castle, page 152. PHOTOGRAPH: the author

PLATE 8

But every day he came back to see the Princess. He shouted at her. He waved his arms at her. He shook his fist at her.

But she shook her head and refused to marry him.

The Wizard had two ugly Goblin Children and he sent them to scare the Princess. They clapped their hands. They danced around and around her. They barked like dogs.

But she still shook her head and refused to marry the Wizard.

Finally the Wizard got very angry. He raised his arms high in the air and shouted "YA YA HABAH." These words cast a magic spell on the Princess so that she was stuck to her chair.

The ugly Goblin Children danced around and around her chair. They pointed their fingers at her and laughed and laughed.

The poor Princess was locked in the top room of the Fantastic Tower and she began to cry.

Then one night Willy the Wise Old Owl flew near the Fantastic Tower and heard the Princess crying.

He also heard the Wizard and the ugly Goblin Children barking like dogs.

So Willy the Wise Old Owl waited outside the tower until the Wizard and the ugly Goblin Children fell asleep. They began to snore.

When Willy heard them snoring, he flew through the window into the Princess's room.

At first she put her hands in front of her face because she was afraid. She thought he was a Wibble-Wabble who worked for the wicked Wizard.

But Willy nodded his head from side to side. And he flapped his wings gently.

The Princess peeped through her fingers.

And when Willy said he wanted to help her, she believed him and she nodded her head to say yes.

She told him that there were four doors to the Tower, but all of them were locked and the wicked Wizard had put the keys in a golden box and buried the box in a garden near a castle in a distant kingdom hundreds of miles away. She pointed a finger to show where the kingdom was.

Willy the Wise Old Owl patted the Princess on her shoulder and comforted her. He promised to fly immediately to the distant kingdom to get the keys and to come back and set her free.

He then nodded his head from side to side and flapped his wings and flew out of the window and away.

He flew over mountains and rivers, on and on, for hundreds of miles, until he came to the distant kingdom and to the Castle of the King.

He flew right into the King's room.

The King jumped up from his chair and shook hands with Willy because everybody knew about the adventures of Willy the Wise Old Owl and the King was very happy to see him.

Willy soon told the King all about the wicked Wizard who was keeping the beautiful Princess a prisoner. He also told him about the four keys which were buried in a golden box in the garden of this very castle. The King decided they must dig up the box and get the keys and then set out that day to rescue the Princess.

The King called his Powerful Servant and they all went out into the garden. The Powerful Servant dug and dug. At last he found the golden box. Inside the box were four keys, one green, one red, one blue, and one golden.

As soon as they had the keys, Willy and the King and the Powerful Servant set out to rescue the Princess.

They leaped onto their horses and galloped away.

After many days and nights, they came at last to the Fantastic Tower. The King took the green key and opened one of the doors.

Out jumped the ugly Red Goblin barking and leaping in the air.

The King clapped his hands once and the Red Goblin disappeared with a terrible howl.

Then the King took the red key and opened another door.

Out jumped the ugly Purple Goblin barking and waving his arms at the King.

But the King clapped his hands twice, and the ugly Purple Goblin groaned and moaned and turned around three times and melted into a puddle of water on the ground.

With the blue key the King opened a third door.

The wicked Wizard jumped out and began stamping his feet like a huge, angry elephant.

This time the Powerful Servant stood in front of the Wizard, raised his arms in the air, and shouted, "ABRA KA CHICKEN SOUP KRA!"

This made the wicked Wizard scream and shake all over. He fell on the ground and never got up again.

Now at last the King took the golden key and opened the last door, expecting to find the Princess inside.

Much to his surprise, a hideous Monster Lady rushed out. She made her hands into claws and scratched the air in front of the King's face, hissing like a wild cat.

This time Willy the Wise Old Owl hooted and flapped his wings at the hideous Monster Lady.

She hopped on one foot and then she hopped on the other foot and then she fell on the ground and turned into a stone.

Finally the King went into the Fantastic Tower, where he found the beautiful Princess.

She was so beautiful that he fell on one knee and begged her to marry him.

Immediately the spell which the wicked Wizard had cast on the Princess was broken and she was free. She got up from her chair, took the King's hand in hers, and nodding her head yes, she agreed to marry him.

The King and the Princess and the Powerful Servant and Willy the Wise Old Owl all joined hands and danced around in a circle for joy.

After the dance, the Princess gave Willy a kiss because she wanted to thank him for helping to rescue her.

Then they all got on a magic carpet and flew back to the King's Castle and Willy flew ahead to show the way.

Once back at the Castle they found a great feast waiting for them [list menu of party] and they all lived happily ever after.

BATTLE FOR THE COSMIC UNIVERSE

INTERGALAXY PANTOMIME WITH MASKS

Stuart R. McLeod
Elizabeth D. Logan

Directions: Read scenario aloud to guests before assigning parts. Specify particular areas in room for each locale: Outer Galaxy, Interspace Station, spot where saucer ship is stranded, Earth, and the Infinite Outer Limits.

Once guests have put on masks, narrator reads each action aloud, allowing actors to interpret by appropriate gestures, movements, and sound effects (no other props are needed), before proceeding to the next development.

CAST OF CHARACTERS IN ORDER OF APPEARANCE

QUASAR WIZARD
PRINCESS OG of the OUTER GALAXY
The QUASAR SLAVE
The I.G.O., an INTERGALAXY OWL
The ABOMINABLE MOLL of the FLYING SAUCERS,
   daughter of the QUASAR WIZARD
HORRIBLE COHORT X, associate of the ABOMINABLE MOLL
KING COSU of the COSMIC UNIVERSE
ASTRONAUT SMITH, from the PLANET EARTH

The Quasar Wizard lures the Princess OG of the Outer Galaxy aboard his Maximum Plosion Gondola by mesmerizing her with magical and mystifying gestures.

He demands that she marry him. She refuses.

The Wizard confides to his Quasar Slave that he plans to vaporize the Princess OG as soon as she is his wife, and then he will have control of all of the Outer Galaxies. Princess OG continues to refuse the Quasar Wizard, despite his threats of torture.

He steers the gondola into Outer Space, making it spin and career. The Princess screams and pleads for him to take her back to her galaxy.

Instead, he carries her to an ISS, a secret Interspace Station, and there he holds her prisoner.

The Quasar Slave dances around her and emits jitter rays to drive her crazy.

As the stellar night sets in, the Wizard presses the Maximum Polar Control Panel button POW in order to send the ISS into sleep orbit. He and the Slave doze off.

But the Princess OG has kept her wits and she resists the sleep orbital pattern.

She extracts the Double Transistor Beam Waver, which she has hidden in her crown, and signals to the other galaxies for help.

But the Quasar Wizard has surrounded the ISS with an oscillation shield which jams the signals. The Princess is in despair and weeps.

An IGO, an Intergalaxy Owl, is searching for Princess OG at the request of King Cosu of the Cosmic Universe. As he explores the neighboring environment, he discovers the ISS and detects the sound of weak distress signals. He is surprised to find an unmapped ISS, and he is even more surprised when he realizes that the signals are being jammed. He circles around the secret Interspace Station. Focusing his Laser Beam Eyes on the ISS, he cuts his way through the Wizard's oscillation shield, enters the ISS, and discovers Princess OG.

At first she is afraid of him, fearing he may be a Malignant Cipher.

But by slowly nodding his head from side to side and fluffing his wings, he reassures her.

He tells her that King Cosu has long loved her and wants her to marry him. This marriage will also unite their spheres of Spatial Influence before the Quasar Wizard can gain control. And even worse, he tells her, the Quasar Wizard is trying to impregnate King Cosu's mind with Radioactive Brain Fumes so that he will marry the Wizard's daughter, the Abominable Moll of the Flying Saucers.

Princess OG thanks the Owl with all her heart, and in order to help him and King Cosu find their way back to her, she gives him half of her Double Transistor Beam Waver. She keeps the other half so that they can zero in on their return trip.

The IGO sets a direct flight pattern for the Planet of the Cosmic Universe.

When he reaches King Cosu, he tells him what the Quasar Wizard has done.

The King listens in horror, is seized with fury, and swears vengeance.

The IGO and King Cosu equip themselves with Ray Guns, Magnetic

Spaceship Trap Nets, and Hyper Torque Gas Ejectors, and together they start out for the ISS in their Supernova Startron Cruiser.

The Quasar Wizard is awakened by the pulsations of the Supernova's engines approaching at the speed of millions of lightyears per second. He throws up a Poison Gas Cloud around the secret Interspace Station.

Princess OG pretends that she is asleep.

As King Cosu and the Intergalaxy Owl approach, the Abominable Moll of the Flying Saucers and her associate Cohort X attack the Supernova Startron Cruiser.

The Abominable Moll tries to Electrify them with Paralyzing Rays from her fingernails.

With powerful Total Spectrum Guns, King Cosu neutralizes the Abominable Moll's Manual Electrical Currents.

Next the Moll and Cohort X attack them with a Spiked Saucer Ship bristling with Space Needles.

King Cosu throws the Magnetic Spaceship Trap Net over the Spiked Saucer.

The Moll and Cohort X are immobilized in the net and are left in the Spiked Saucer Ship, derelict in space, jibbering in unknown tongues.

King Cosu and the Intergalaxy Owl approach the ISS and polarize the Poison Gas Cloud with their Hyper Torque Gas Ejectors.

Entering the ISS, King Cosu and the IGO Galvanize the Quasar Wizard and his Slave with Stellatic Dust.

The Princess bows to King Cosu and thanks him for rescuing her.

In the meantime, back at the Spiked Saucer Ship, the Abominable Moll has dissolved the Magnetic Spaceship Trap Net with pulsations from her Supercharged Cataclystic Hair. She and Cohort X rush to the ISS and freeze the complete station, including the Wizard and his Slave, as well as Princess OG, King Cosu, and the IGO.

From the planet Earth, Astronaut Smith, who has strayed off course, by chance steers his Fugitive Module to the ISS. The Moll attacks the module, but Astronaut Smith, equipped as he is with the FWP Composite Surveyor Thermonuclear Control Panel, vaporizes the Moll and Cohort X with one blast from Push Button 12.

Then with a Hyper Sensitive Detector, he is able to distinguish the good people and the evil people among the frozen inmates of the ISS.

Very carefully, he thaws out the King, the Princess, and the Owl.

Slowly and painfully they begin to move, first their fingers, then their hands and feet, then arms and legs, and finally their whole bodies.

Smith helps them aboard his Fugitive Module.

He restores their strength by giving them shots of Aqueous Dehydrated Elixir.

With one touch of his finger to Button 17, Astronaut Smith Etherizes the entire ISS, the Quasar Wizard, and the Space Slave into a Cyclonic Mist.

As the mist is blown away by Protoscopic Gales into the Infinite Outer Limits, the fading howls and cries of the Wizard and his Slave drift back to the module.

Astronaut Smith uses the Double Transistor Beam Waver to guide the module to Princess OG's Outer Galaxy Territories for the Royal Wedding.

A great and sumptuous feast is spread of [list the menu for the party], toasts are drunk, and all live happily ever after.

LARGE CASTLE

(See jacket. Cut out colored picture and tip in back of book with magic mending tape.)

The parts of this centerpiece are separate. After the party they can be rearranged in a number of ways and used as a toy village. More parts can also be added later.

Do not try to duplicate the castle exactly, but improvise and elaborate with the materials you have at hand.

For a birthday party, bake a cake in a square or rectangular pan and cut into rectangular blocks to make towers. Set towers on end and ice individually with different colored icing. Make windows, gates, and parapet of icing, candies, and cake decorations. Cover top of cake stand with layer of royal icing and set towers in it while it is wet. It will act as glue to keep them upright, in place. Stick birthday candles in tops of towers, or make flags (see page 151) to stick in top of towers.

MATERIALS

cardboard boxes
  cylindrical:
    oatmeal box
    salt box
    scouring powder box
    cotton balls box
  rectangular
mailing tubes
paper towel cores
paper cups
plain and figured gift-wrapping
  paper
shelf paper
flocked velour paper
newspaper
tissue paper
2- and 3-ply bristol board
cardboard, heavy and lightweight
plain and striped glossy gift-
  wrapping ribbon

steel washers
dressmaker's braids and metallic
  cords
gilt paint
corsage pins
salt, buckshot, nuts, and bolts,
  etc.
green-enameled florist wire
map tacks
fine nibbed felt-tipped marking
  pens
beads
gum-backed stars
large fat candles
staples
Scotch, double-stick, and masking
  tapes
rubber cement
Sobo and Uhu glue
straight pins

Photograph from *House & Garden* by Fotiades and Miehlmann; copyright © 1965 by Condé Nast Publications Inc.

Paper for
base plan

1. Lay strips of shelf paper side by side, edges overlapping, to make an area a little larger than you want your castle to cover. Tape edges together, being careful to keep paper flat. Lay this on the table before you begin to work.

To make
arrangement
on paper

2. Assemble a large variety of boxes, towel cores, and tubes. Arrange them on the paper in a number of ways until you find one that pleases you.

To make plan

3. On the shelf paper, draw around each box, core, and tube as a reminder of the arrangement. Key the outlines on the paper with the corresponding box, core, or tube. Use numbers or letters placed on the bottom of the boxes and inside the lower edge of the tubes and cores.

To cut
cylindrical boxes
and boards

4. To assure a straight line, cut cylindrical boxes with a saw and miter box. Sand edges clean. Cut cardboard with a safety razor blade and a metal-edged ruler. Cut paper and bristol board with scissors and pinking or scallop shears.

To strengthen
buildings

5. To make buildings and walls stronger, stuff boxes with crushed newspapers. Secure ends with masking tape.

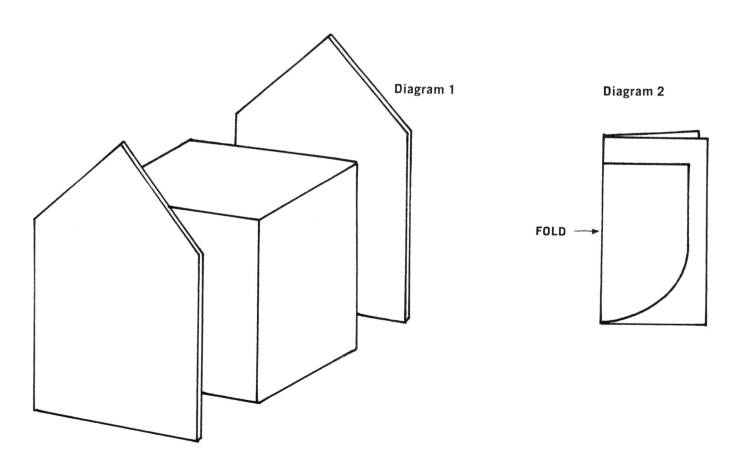

Diagram 1

Diagram 2

FOLD →

6. Combine 2 or more boxes to get a shape or size you do not have. Strip boxes together with masking tape. Be generous with tape to make strong and solid shapes.

To combine small boxes

7. To make a gabled roof, follow diagram 1. Cut 2, one for each end of building. Glue and tape to box.

To cut gable ends and roofs

Cut roof one inch larger on bottom and side edges, but *not* on top edges, of gable. Join 2 sides along top with masking tape.

8. To keep tall, thin towers from tipping over, cut a circle of cardboard to fit under base. Glue steel washers, preferably just large enough to fit inside tower, to cardboard. Glue cardboard to base of tower.

To keep tall tower upright

9. Use pointed paper cups to make the conical roofs. If you have no cups of the proper size, cut a semicircle of 2-ply bristol board. Roll it into a cone. Secure the edges with tape. Use a spring clothespin to hold cone together while you tape it. Stuff cup or cone with glue-dabbed tissue paper.

Conical roof

10. Cut circle of colored paper 1 inch wider than diameter of tower. Fringe edge $\frac{1}{2}$ inch, cement paper over top of box, press down fringe, and cement to its sides. Measure circumference of box with a tape measure and cut strip of 3-ply bristol board 1 inch longer than circumference and $1\frac{1}{2}$ inches higher than tower.

Round crenellated tower

Divide circumference into 12 or 14 equal parts, draw line $\frac{1}{2}$ inch from top edge, and cut out crenellations. Attach one end of board to tower with masking tape. Tape along entire height of tower and edge of board. Roll board tightly around tower and tape other end down its complete length.

11. Cut a strip of paper the height of tower and its crenellation and 1 inch longer than its girth. Attach one end of paper to tower with Scotch tape. Cement the paper in place, or place a number of short, overlapping strips of double-stick tape on the underside of the loose end. Roll paper tightly around tower and carefully take or press end in place.

To cover crenellated tower

12. Cut a strip of paper—matching or contrasting—to the outside, 1 inch longer than circumference, $1\frac{3}{4}$ inches wide, and cement in place. Press tightly against crenellations and be sure that it does not pull away from them.

To cover inside of crenellation

When dry, carefully cut around bristol board, leaving about $\frac{1}{16}$ inch of paper outside the board to hide its edges.

Line edge between tower top and inside wall with metallic cord.

To weight candle stands

13. Make candle stands of cylindrical boxes, such as scouring powder cans. Weight them with salt, buck shot, bolts and nuts, or any small heavy objects. Be sure that the cans are too heavy to tip over when a large candle is placed on top. Tape opening in top closed.

Cover top of can with circle of cardboard; glue in place. Complete by following the directions for the round crenellated tower (directions 10, 11, and 12). Omit metallic cord. You may want to cover the roof and line the crenellations with black.

Walls

14. Cut rectangle of paper 1 inch longer and wider than top of wall, miter corners, and cement over top. Fringe edges and cement to top of walls. Cut strip of paper the girth of walls and 1 inch wider than height. The latter is to turn under and cement to bottom of wall. Fold paper around wall and crease along edges, arranging so that end of paper coincides with a corner. Miter the corners where the paper will be folded under the wall. Cement paper in place over walls or attach with double-stick tape as on round crenellated tower. Fold under edges and cement or tape in place.

Square crenellated tower

15. To cover, follow directions as for walls. To make crenellation, cut 3 strips of ribbon 1 inch longer than circumference and cement together.

Carefully crease ribbon to fit around corners. Divide each side into 10 equal parts and cut out crenellations. Cement in place and cover lower edge with braid.

Buildings

16. Glue and tape gable ends in place. When dry, cover building with paper. Cut strip 1 inch longer than circumference of building and with a width the height of gable plus 1 inch to turn under the bottom. Fit paper around building. Cut away excess paper from edges of gable ends and tops of side walls. Attach paper to building either with cement or Scotch and double-stick tapes as in direction 11.

Rectangular roofs

17. Cut paper 1 inch larger on all sides than roof. Cement in place. Bend roof along ridge pole. Crease paper along edges of roof. Miter corners and fold paper under roof. Cement and tape in place.

18. Draw semicircles 1 inch longer than radii of cone on *back* of paper. Cut out with scissors or pinking or scallop shears. Cement or tape over cone.

Conical roofs

19. Glue roofs in place by running a line of glue along edge of building. When tacky, set roof on it and press down. Be sure that each roof projects an equal amount over gable ends and that conical roofs are not tilted.

To attach roof

20. Make parts of gatehouse first: 2 large round towers with conical roofs and a thin, rectangular building. Cover parts with paper; glue roofs in place.

Gatehouse

Cement arches of paper for gateway opening and door to center building. Draw in portcullis with marking pen. Outline arched opening with looped braid (see below).

21. Cut rectangle of cardboard for drawbridge. Cover with paper. Pin and glue ends of metallic cord to underside at front corners. Set bridge in place. Pull cords taut and mark points on cord. Cut cord $\frac{1}{8}$ inch longer than marks. Glue ends to side of arch. When dry, glue small gold bead or map tack over each joint. Attach bridge on underside to bottom of building with Scotch tape.

Drawbridge

22. Glue towers and central building together. Brace between heavy uprights overnight.

To join parts of gatehouse

23. Trim buildings with dressmaker's braids. Add a drop of Sobo glue to freshly cut ends of braid to keep them from raveling. If white string inside braid shows when glue is dry, cover it with gilt paint.

Trimmings

Braid on walk above gateway is held erect by straight pins. Glue them upright in the braid, the points stuck into the building.

24. Draw tiles on some roofs, stones on round crenellated tower and candle stands with marking pens. Note that only clusters of tiles and stones are used. As a variation, cover one tower or building completely with stones or one roof with tiles.

Tiles and stones

25. Make flags by folding strips of ribbon in half and covering one inner side with cement. Run fine line of glue along inside of crease and place corsage pin or florist wire in it. Allow wire to protrude $\frac{1}{2}$ inch

Flags

above ribbon. Press ribbon together, allow to dry, pressing flat occasionally. Cut ends into 2 long points. Glue beads to top of wire (see diagrams, page 151).

To attach flags   26. Pierce points of conical roofs and the tissue inside with a darning needle. Insert wire and pin poles with drops of glue.

To assemble castle   27. Arrange parts of castle on plan, matching keys. Transfer to flocked velour paper. Draw around outside of castle. Remove building and cut flocked paper about $3/16$ inch *inside* lines. Replace buildings with flocked paper for the courtyard.

If castle is to be stored for even a few days before displaying, it is wise to keep the plan, too. You may be surprised at how quickly you can forget where each part goes.

Napkin rings   28. Cement 3 strips of ribbon one on top of another. Use 2 strips 6 inches long and 1 strip $6\frac{1}{2}$ inches long. Cement longest piece on outside with $\frac{1}{2}$ inch exposed at one end. Divide top edge into $\frac{1}{2}$-inch sections, cut out crenellations, curving ribbon as you work. When dry, remove excess cement. Join ends, overlapping the $\frac{1}{2}$-inch single thickness and cement in place.

Place cards   29. Cut patterns for place cards from piece of folded shelf paper (see diagram 2, page 144). Transfer to 3-ply bristol board and cut out. Score down center and fold. Cover and decorate with paper as in photograph. Write name with marking pen.

SMALL CASTLE

This, like the Large Castle and the following Tin Can Castle, can be used as a centerpiece for either an adults' or children's party, or for a dinner or buffet table. Set it on the hall or living room table for a party or for the duration of a festive holiday.

Follow photograph as guide to directions.

MATERIALS

rectangular cardboard boxes	gift-wrapping metallic ribbon
large, very shallow, rectangular cardboard box	gift-wrapping metallic cord
	beads
round salt or oatmeal box	green-enameled florist wire
towel cores	corsage pins
newspaper	staples
masking tape	rubber cement
1-ply bristol board	Uhu glue
gift-wrapping paper	cord

1. Stuff boxes with crushed newspaper and tape tightly closed. Stuff the ends of the towel cores with glue-dabbed crushed newspaper. To make a flat base on core, press one end against a flat surface until glue is dry.

To strengthen boxes

2. Arrange boxes in an interesting combination on shallow box and mark their positions.

Arrangement

3. Cement paper to either side of pieces of bristol board. Cut out strips with scallop or pinking shears for two rectangular buildings, as in photograph. Cut a wider strip into large points for the round buildings. Glue in place and trim with ribbons.

Crenellation

4. Make cones of semicircles of bristol board. Overlap ends, staple, and tape together.

Use pinking shears to cut out paper semicircles, with 1-inch radii longer than those of bristol-board cones. Cement paper over cones.

Stuff cones with glue-dabbed crushed newspaper. Glue to tops of towers.

Roofs

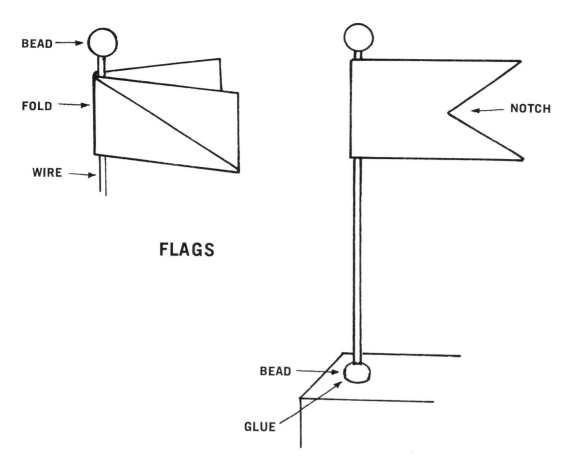

FLAGS

5. Use scallop or pinking shears to cut out rectangles for gateway. Decorate with holes cut with paper punch. Make door and windows from rectangles of ribbon. Decorate windows on round building with bits of cord.

Door and windows

6. Make flags from strips of paper, folded in half, and glued together around corsage pins and wires. Leave enough wire above flag to glue on beads. Notch ends of flags and trim with bits of paper and ribbon.

Flags

7. Punch holes in flat roofs. Slip beads over bottom ends of wire, insert ends into holes, each with a drop of glue. Punch corsage pins into the tips of conical roof.

To attach flagpoles

8. Arrange buildings on base. Trace around them with fine hard pencil point. Glue in place.

To assemble

(See color plate 8.) # TIN CAN CASTLE

Children old enough to be careful when handling the cut tin tops may use this for play.

MATERIALS

tin cans
small foil pans
newspaper
corrugated box 8 x 10¼ x 4 inches
   (ours is a 30-pad Brillo box)
heavy-duty kitchen aluminum foil
2-ply bristol board
dressmaker's tapes, novelty
   embroideries, ruching, butterfly
   ruffling, woven bands, fringed
   cotton-knit trim, Venice-lace
   and gold and silver braid
   beads

liquid textile dye
Color-Aid or other brightly
   colored heavy paper
large balls from curtain fringe
iridescent Christmas tree balls
⅜-inch plywood board 19 x 25 inches
miniature evergreens and trees
rubber cement
staples
Sobo and Uhu glue
Scotch, Mystic, and invisible
   mending tapes

You will need a pair of long-nose pliers to curl the tin and a pair of tin shears to cut it. If possible, beg, borrow, or buy a pair of shears with compound leverage. These will make the work easier and faster.

Always wear heavy work gloves when cutting. Do *not* allow small children in the room until all your metal cutting has been completed, your work has been put away, and the floor and work surfaces have been cleaned. Small slivers of metal may be wiped up with a wet paper towel.

To collect and prepare cans

1. Collect cans of various sizes and shapes. Use a sardine or smoked oyster can for gate 5, and a rectangular olive oil can for gatehouse 6. The other cans should be round with paper labels that can be soaked off.

2. Wash and polish the round cans with soap and steel wool.

3. In order to make a large surface for gluing the tin cans together, crush newspapers and dab with Sobo glue. Stuff each can with this. Flatten the paper level with the top of the can.

Towers 4 and 12 have large bases. The lower cans may be trimmed as battlements as on tower 12.

4. When glue is dry, use Uhu to glue cans together to form towers.

5. Follow diagrams A and B (page 157) to make cut-tin decorations for the top of tower 1. *Tower tops*

      A. Use $4\frac{1}{4}$-inch-high can. Fringe top into $\frac{1}{4}$-inch-wide strips, 2 inches deep.

      B. Hold tip of each strip with pliers and curl strip. Vary the length of curls on 3 successive strips.

6. For tower 3 use a $4\frac{1}{4}$-inch-diameter can top and cut into a swirl as in C. Bend each swirl upright and turn at right angles to sides to form open dome as in D.

7. For tower 4, cut another $4\frac{1}{4}$-inch-diameter top in swirls as in C and bend swirls upright. Curl ends to flare outward as in E.

8. For tower 13, cut $4\frac{1}{4}$-inch-diameter can top in swirls as in D. Use Uhu to glue an iridescent ball in center and glue a large pearl bead on top of ball.

Glue circle of colored paper on an inverted foil pan. Glue dome to it. Set on second foil pan with the same size rim and straighter sides, as in photograph and drawing. Glue pans together.

9. Fringe the rim of a foil pan into $\frac{1}{8}$-inch strips as in F. Curl and twist ends with pliers for 12.

10. For roofs, cut semicircles of bristol board or paper. Form into cones (see item 18, page 27) held with staples and invisible mending tape. Make 2 roofs to fit inside tops made for towers 4 and 12. Make other roofs wide enough to fit over and project well beyond top edge of towers. *Roofs*

11. For square building 7 (Brillo box), cut a sheet of aluminum foil large enough to cover it. Paint foil with liquid dye and allow to dry overnight. *Square building 7*

12. Stuff cardboard box 7, with glue-dabbed newspaper for greater strength. Hold box tightly shut with Scotch tape.

13. Cover box with dyed foil. Use rubber cement. Be sure that foil is held firmly in place and stretched tightly over one side of box before covering the next side.

14. To make base, edge plywood rectangle with Mystic tape. Use rubber cement to cover board with colored paper. Be sure paper is at- *Base*

tached uniformly and completely over the entire board so that towers can be glued securely to it.

15. Before completing towers and box, arrange on board, set roofs, gate, and gatehouse in place and check proportions.

To decorate towers

16. Glue decorations around tower sides, over seams that join cans. Use woven trims, Venice lace, gold braids, and novelty embroideries. Both Sobo and Uhu can be used for this, but on the fabrics, Sobo usually works better. Allow it to stand on the fabric until tacky before applying the fabric to the metal.

To attach tops to towers

17. Use Uhu to attach cut tin tops to towers.
   a. For tower 1, glue top in diagram A and B in place and cover seam with daisy lace.
   b. For tower 3, glue top in diagram D and cover joint with butterfly ruffling.
   c. For tower 4, attach top in diagram E.
   d. For tower 12, attach top in diagram F and glue line of bead dangle braid beneath it.
   e. For tower 13, glue pans and top (step 8) to a 7-inch-high can with a $4\frac{1}{4}$-inch diameter. Trim rim of top pan with row of beads. Cover seam with pearl beads on tape.

Decorations on roofs and buildings

18. Decorate edge of roof of tower 9 as in G and H. Decorate edges of roofs of towers 2, 8 and 11 with braids and embroideries as in photograph and drawing.

19. Decorate top of building 7 with dressmaker's jeweled trim and glue a Venice-lace daisy to center above gate. Glue braid around top of tower 10.

20. Trim gatehouse 6 with ruching, woven trim, and bead dangle braid.

21. Cut an oblong of colored paper and cement inside sardine can 5 for door. Trim door with rhinestone strips, use Uhu to attach. Use Sobo to glue butterfly ruffling around edge of can on 3 sides.

To attach roofs, and balls to roof points

22. Use Uhu to glue roofs to towers and to glue iridescent balls and curtain-fringe balls to pointed roofs.

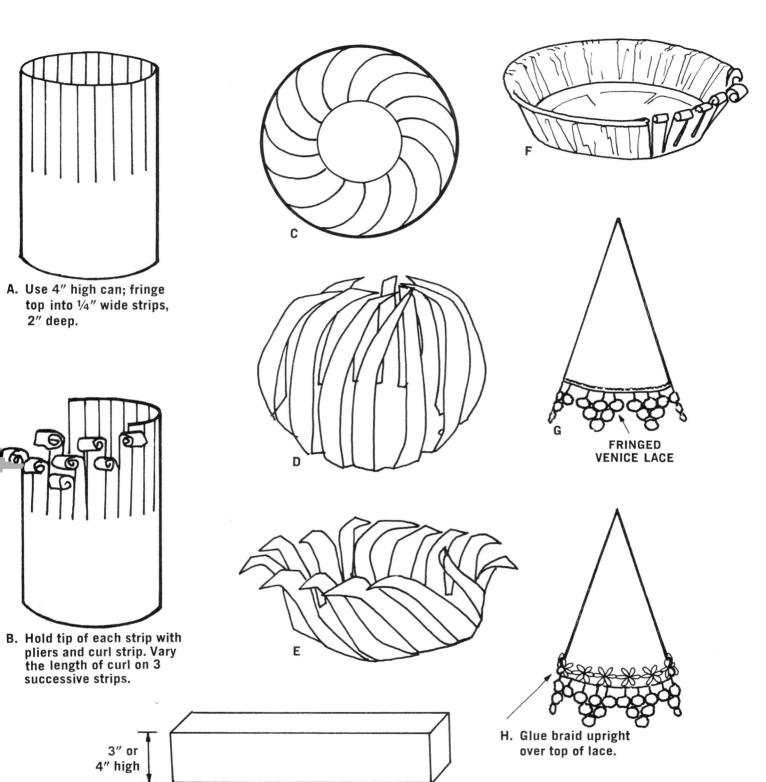

A. Use 4″ high can; fringe top into ¼″ wide strips, 2″ deep.

B. Hold tip of each strip with pliers and curl strip. Vary the length of curl on 3 successive strips.

C.

D.

E.

F.

G.

FRINGED VENICE LACE

H. Glue braid upright over top of lace.

3″ or 4″ high

I. Wall

To assemble castle 23. To mark final locations, arrange cans on base. Use a pencil to trace around gate, gatehouse, central building, and towers. Glue them in place.

Path and landscaping 24. Cut fringe from cotton-knit trim for the path and glue in place.

25. Glue small Venice-lace daisies on base. Add trees and evergreens. These can be attached with Uhu or merely set in place.

Castle for play 26. If children would like a larger building with a courtyard for soldiers and other figures, remove the buildings piece by piece from the base.

Walls 27. Collect long, rectangular boxes 3 or 4 inches high to use for walls as in I.

28. Cut sheets of foil large enough to cover each box. Paint with fabric dye, using a different color for each wall.

29. Cement foil over walls. Trim top edges with braids, embroideries, etc. The walls should be placed in a circle with towers between them to form the exterior of the castle. The gate and gatehouse should be placed between the 2 center walls at the front and the rectangular building and remaining towers in the center of the courtyard for the keep.

30. Pieces can be left separate for children to arrange them in changing combinations. Or they can be remounted. In either case, cut a piece of $\frac{1}{2}$-inch plywood 2 or 3 times the size of the original base. Edge board with tape and cover with paper as in direction 13. Follow directions 23, 24, and 25 to complete.

ALTERNATES OR SUBSTITUTIONS

1. Use old gift-wrapping paper, colored or decorated, to cover building 7 and walls.

2. Use pieces of ribbon for paths and as decorations around tower seams.

3. For trees, spray bottle brushes with green paint, cut the handle short, and insert in blocks of wood or soap.

PROJECTS III

Gifts for All Ages

GIFT-WRAPPED PACKAGES FOR CHILDREN

Dimensions are given for the boxes shown, but plan to adapt these to the measurements of the boxes you have available.

MATERIALS

gift-wrapping paper
gift-wrapping glossy and
    metallic ribbon
gift-wrapping metallic cord
sequins
1- and 2-ply bristol board
gift-wrapping yarn

notarial seals
heavy thread
felt-tipped marking pens
double-stick, Scotch, and
    invisible mending tape
Uhu glue
rubber cement

Wrap boxes in paper and secure flaps with tapes. Enlarge patterns by square (see page 24, item 12).

Gingerbread Boy (3 x 6½ x 6¼ inches)

To cover box

1. Cover box with gold-spattered paper.

Figure

2. Cut figure from 2-ply bristol board, pattern page 166. Cement dark green or brown foil paper over it, leaving a generous margin around figure. Fringe margin, fold under, and cement to back of figure.

Features and trimmings

3. Pull string from inside gold cord and iron flat. Cut strips of empty flat cord and glue in place on costume and for hair. Cut small strip and curve between fingers for mouth. Cut off excess cord at edges of figure. Glue sequin eyes and buttons in place.
Make a bow of glossy ribbon and glue to top of head.

To attach

4. Attach to box with rubber cement.

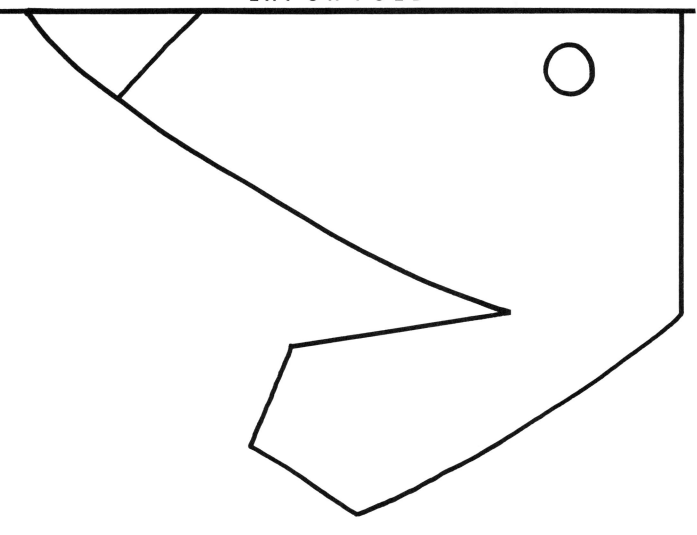

Reindeer ($7\frac{1}{4}$ x $7\frac{1}{2}$ x $7\frac{1}{2}$ inches)

To cover box   1. Cover box with gold foil paper.

Patterns   2. Cut patterns from 2-ply bristol board.

Head   3. Cement purple paper on head and pink on nose. Glue gold notarial seals in place for eyes. Fold head down center.

Antlers   4. Cut antlers from 2-ply bristol board. Fold on dotted line and glue to box, as in photograph.

ANTLERS
Cut 2.

5. Make pompom of pink yarn (see page 29, item 27). Glue in place.

Bangs

6. Use double-stick tape on either side of top of head. Be sure that center fold projects ½ inch or more from box before pressing sides of head firmly against box.

To attach head

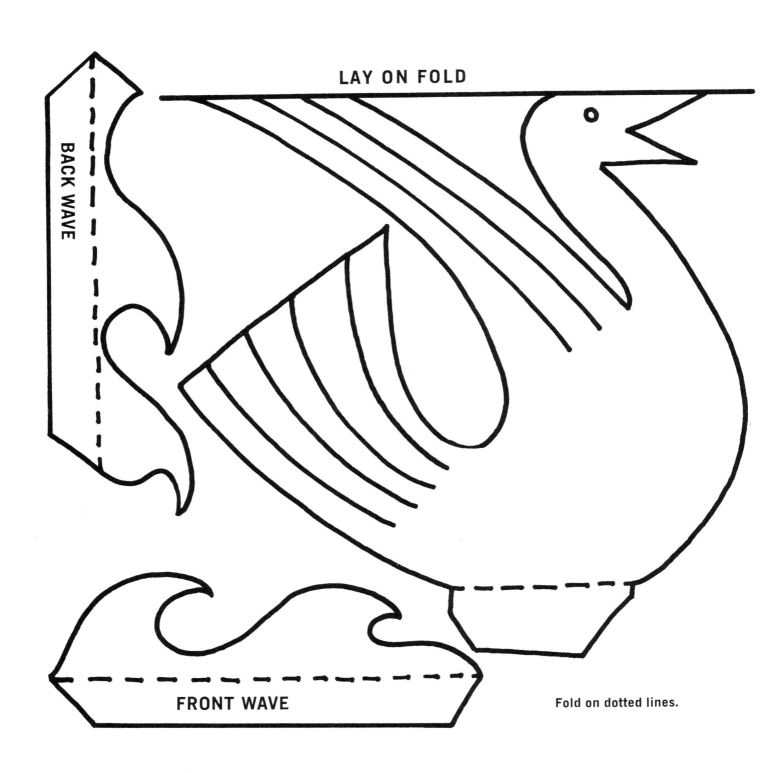

BACK WAVE

LAY ON FOLD

FRONT WAVE

Fold on dotted lines.

Bird (4¼ x 4¼ x 4½ inches)

1. Cover box with green and blue paper with a wavy pattern. *To cover box*

2. Fold 1-ply bristol board; lay pattern, opposite page, on fold as indicated and cut out. Draw eyes and curved lines on wings and tail with marking pens. Fold on dotted lines. *Bird*
   Glue heads, necks, tips of wings, and tails together. Fold under flaps at base, overlap, and glue together so that bird will stand upright. Glue to box.

3. Cement 2 strips of paper 1¾ x 24 inches back to back. Trace and cut out waves. Fold on dotted line. Cut 3 lines of waves to go in front of bird and 1 to go behind. Cement to box top. *Waves*

4. Attach 2 bands of ribbon around box with double-stick tape. *Ribbon*

Clown (2 x 3¾ x 14¼ inches)

1. Wrap box in polka-dot paper. *To cover box*

2. Cut a strip of 1-ply board 4½ inches deep and long enough to wrap around box. Patterns are on page 166. Cut gloves from same board. Use markers to draw face on strip and lines on gloves. Cement strips around top of box, centering face on front. Bend corners of gloves around edges of box and glue to it. Leave thumb, fingers, and most of palm free to stand away from surface. *Head and gloves*

3. Cut feet from 2-ply board and cement purple paper over them. Glue feet to bottom of box as in photograph. *Feet*

4. See item 28, fourth row, page 31–32. Cut 24 pieces of yarn, varying in length from 3 to 8 inches. Tie bundle in center with thread and glue to top of box. Cut off enough front ends so that face will show. Glue clippings to center of head. *Hair*

5. Unravel 2 short pieces of yarn and glue to shoes for pompoms. *Pompoms*

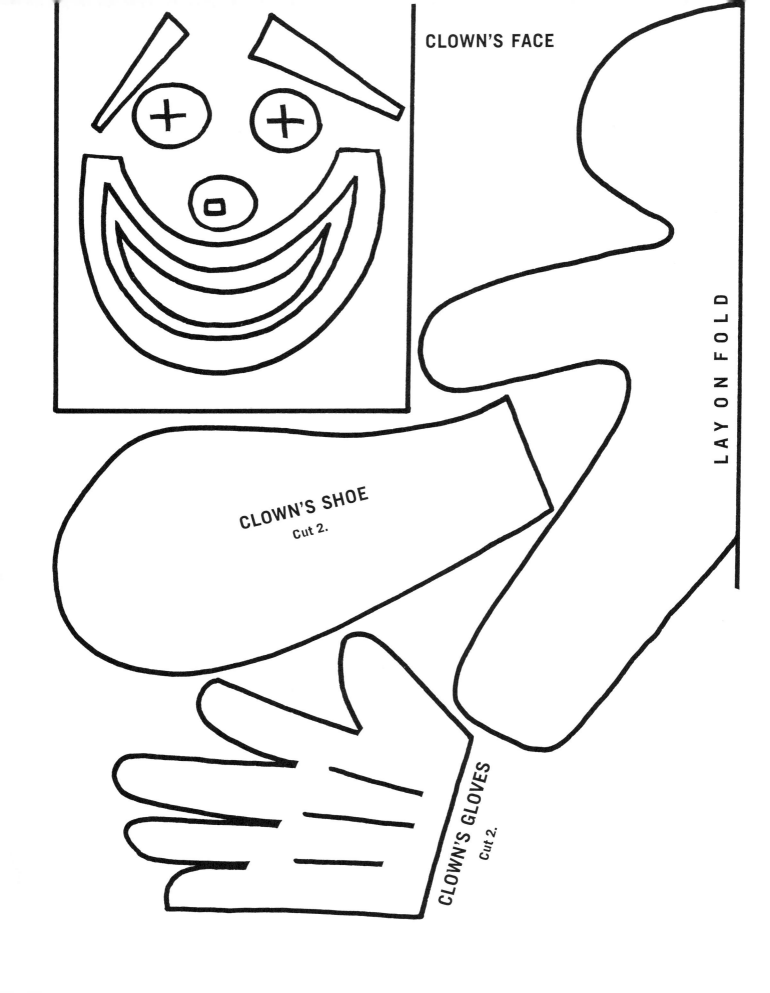

CLOWN'S FACE

LAY ON FOLD

CLOWN'S SHOE
Cut 2.

CLOWN'S GLOVES
Cut 2.

Candy Decorated Church, page 84. Reprinted from *Better Homes and Gardens*

PLATE 9

Shell Bouquet in Shadow Box, page 223. PHOTOGRAPH: the author

PLATE 10

Mirror in Shell Decorated Frame, page 221
PHOTOGRAPH: the author

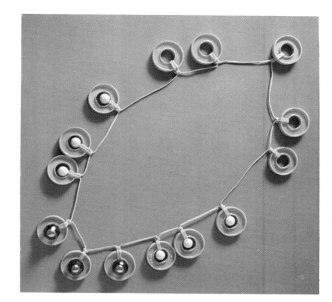

Necklace I, page 228. PHOTOGRAPH: the author

Necklace III, page 233. PHOTOGRAPH: the author

PLATE 11

Figures with Curtain-Fringe Ball Heads,
page 58. PHOTOGRAPH: the author

Burlap "Embroidery," page 190
PHOTOGRAPH: the author

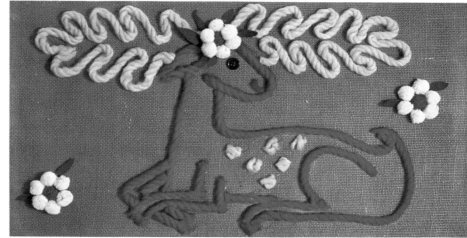

PLATE 12

Drawer Box, page 179. PHOTOGRAPH: Ray Porter, reprinted from *Seventeen*

Letter Box, page 182. PHOTOGRAPH: Ray Porter, reprinted from *Seventeen*

Picture Frame Box, page 174. PHOTOGRAPH: Ray Porter, reprinted from *Seventeen*

PLATE 13

Egg Shell Mosaic Plaque, page 188. PHOTOGRAPH: the author

PLATE 14

Collage, page 193. PHOTOGRAPH: the author

PLATE 15

Makeup Box, page 175. PHOTOGRAPH: Ray Porter, reprinted from *Seventeen*

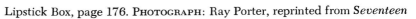

Lipstick Box, page 176. PHOTOGRAPH: Ray Porter, reprinted from *Seventeen*

PLATE 16

GIFT BOXES

1. To make doors, lay a box on a piece of cardboard, with open side down. Draw outline of box on cardboard. With a ruler, draw a line down center; cut out the 2 doors.

Doors

2. Use wide plastic tape, one strip on the inside of the box, one on the outside.

Hinges

3. To glue cord, braid, fringe, etc., first apply a line of glue to the box with a toothpick. Allow glue to set until tacky, about a minute. Lay trimming on it and press down. Use a toothpick to manipulate trimming around corners and curves.

To glue cord in place

4. Apply glue with a toothpick to small pieces of fabric or paper or to small objects. Use a pair of tweezers to put these in place. Bent tweezers, such as dentists use, are the best.

Small trimmings, etc.

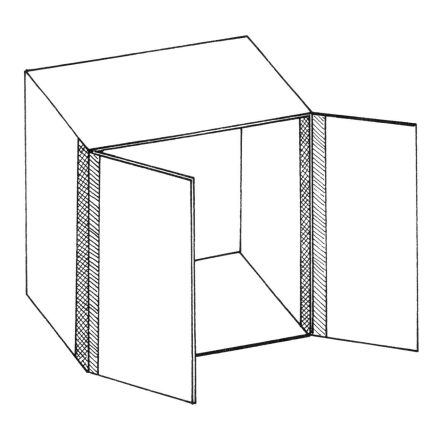

Yarn Caddy

MATERIALS

8½-inch-high cylindrical box
large Styrofoam ball
pipe cleaner
heavy yarn
felt

yarn markers or metal eyelets
lipstick
curtain-fringe balls
Sobo glue

1. Use an 8½-inch-high cylindrical box. Punch hole in center of lid with ice pick. Cut large Styrofoam ball in half, punch hole through center, and glue to lid with Sobo.

Loop heavy yellow pipe cleaner and insert through hole in Styrofoam and lid. Tie ends in large knot so that by holding the loop you can lift and replace the lid.

2. Wind and glue yarn around edge of lid and lower part of Styrofoam.

Loop yarn, about one-third of a small skein at a time, around carton. Tie strands together with piece of yarn, slip from carton and cut strands to form tassel (see diagram, page 29, item 27). Pin and glue 5 or 6 of these to head for hair.

Make 2 more, half the size of the others, for bangs.

Reprinted from *Seventeen*

3. Cover carton with felt, glued on with Sobo. Cut bottom of neck with scallop or pinking shears.

4. Punch holes for eyes and nose; enlarge enough to fit yarn markers in them. Glue markers in place with Sobo.

5. Cut mouth and bow of felt. Glue bow to hair and pipe cleaner.

6. Rouge cheeks with 2 shades of lipstick.

7. Glue balls from curtain fringe around neck.

8. Fill caddy with yarn and insert 3 different colors through the eyes and nose.

Bangle Box

MATERIALS

box	yarn
heavy cardboard	signal dots
plastic and masking tape	gold-embossed paper cut-out
colored paper	circles
paper-towel core	lipstick or red pencil
Styrofoam rectangles	Uhu and Sobo glue
braid	Duco cement
bead	rubber cement

1. Use a long, narrow box. Reinforce with heavy cardboard. Make door and hinge at top. Use plastic tape to bind all edges of box and door. *Box and door*

2. Cement paper panels to sides, back, top, and bottom of box and to door. Line box. *To cover*

3. Make post from paper-towel core. Cut it short enough to allow ample room for placing and removing bangles. *Post and base*

4. Cut Styrofoam rectangle for base to fit in bottom of box. Cut hole in center to insert post.

5. Cover post with paper and decorate with braid. Cover base with plastic tape and paper. Glue post into base with Sobo. Glue base in box with Sobo.

Door   6. Use Uhu to glue bead to bottom of door for handle.

Head   7. Trace pattern and cut out parts. Cement head and stand to door. Make hair of yarn, eyes of signal dots, and jewelry of gold-embossed paper cut-out rings. Turn gold on rings to silver by wiping rings with a bit of cotton and a drop of Duco cement. Rouge cheeks with lipstick or red pencil.

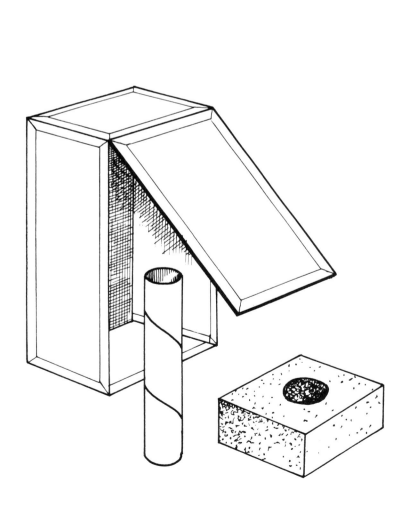

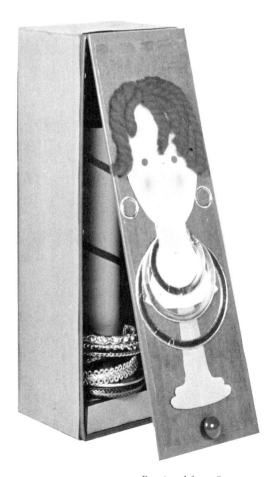

Reprinted from *Seventeen*

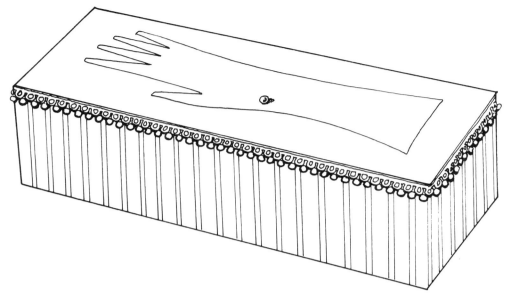

Glove Box

MATERIALS

box	pearl button
plain and striped paper	rubber cement
straight pins	Uhu glue
2-ply bristol board	braid

1. Cover box. Attach small ball-fringed braid around edge; hold in place with pins until dry.

2. Trace pattern and cut glove from bristol board, cement in place, and glue pearl button at wrist.

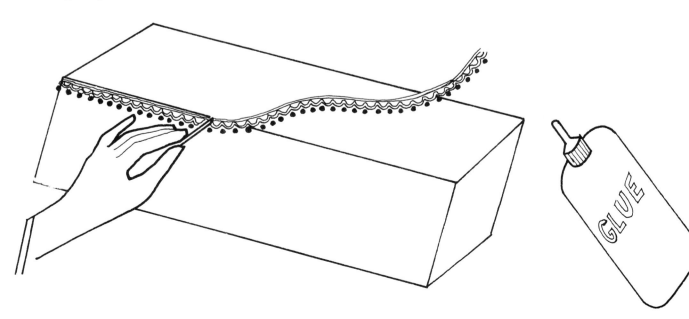

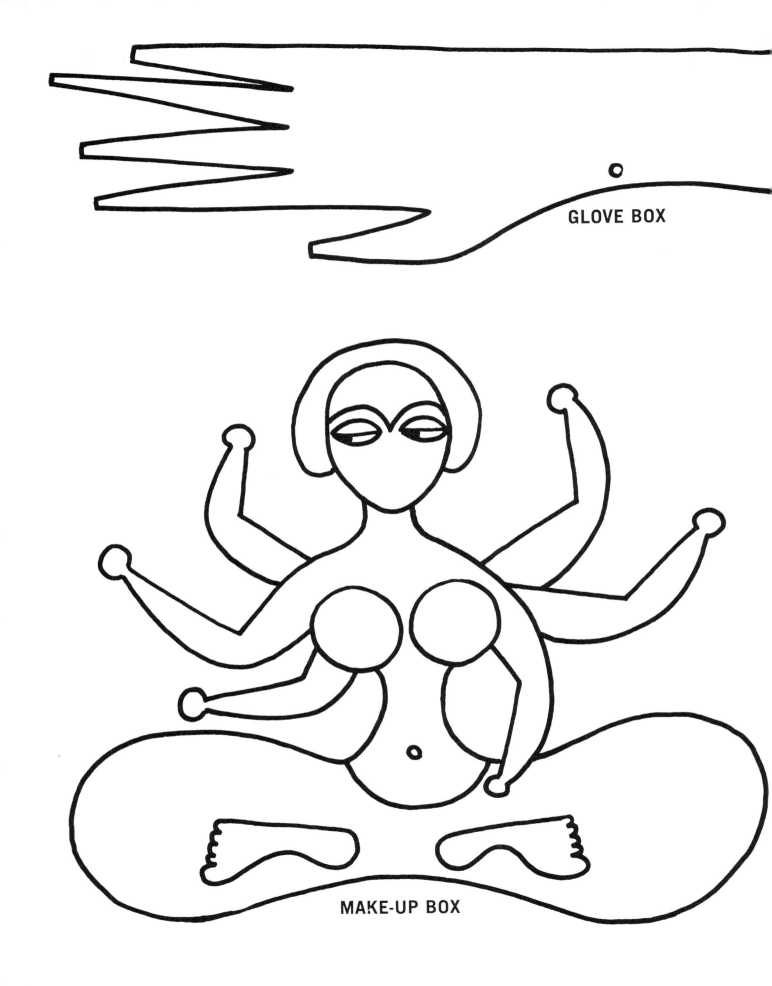

GLOVE BOX

MAKE-UP BOX

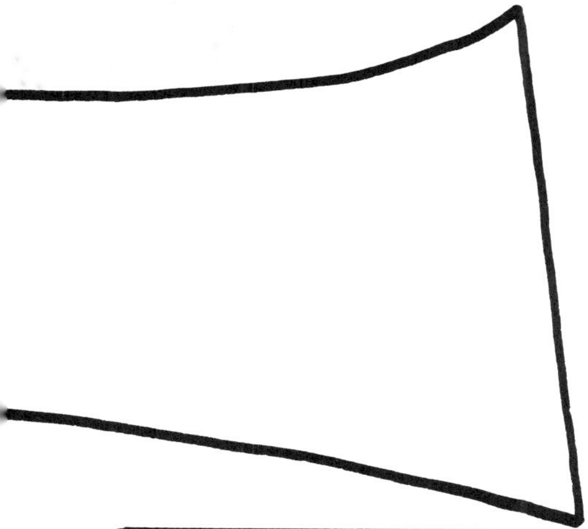

BANGLE BOX

PICTURE FRAME BOX

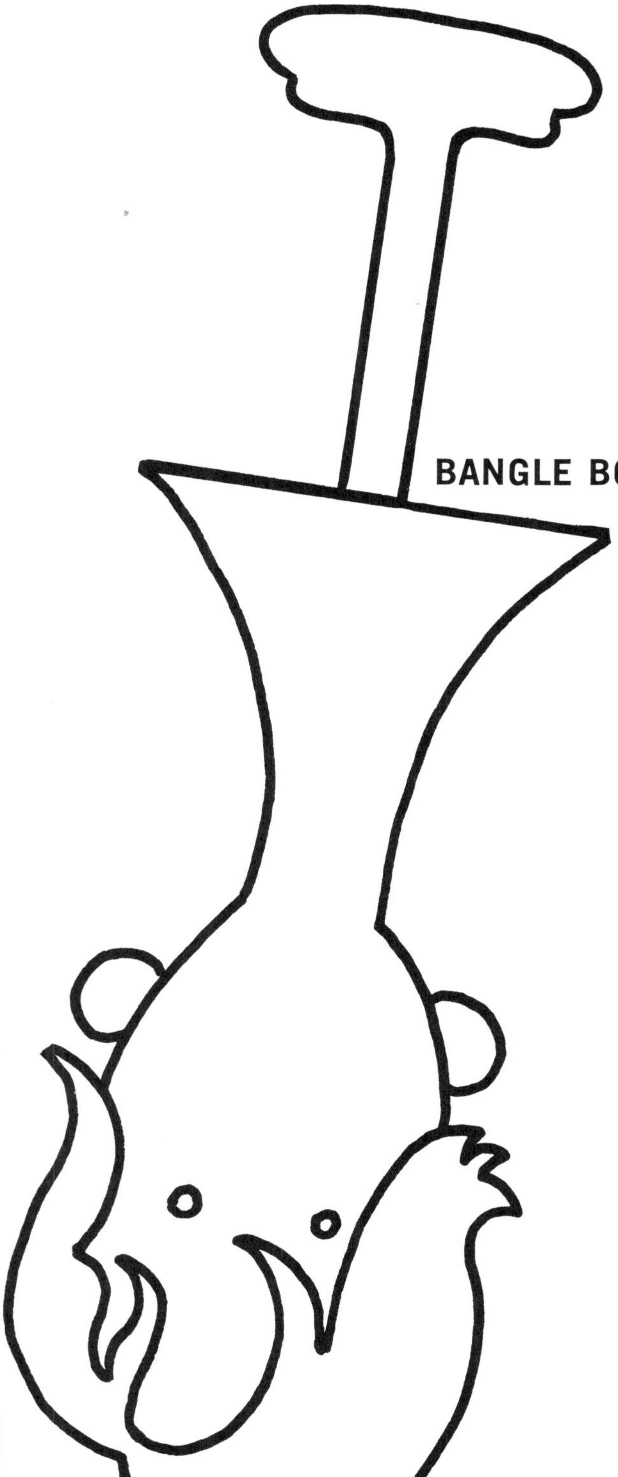

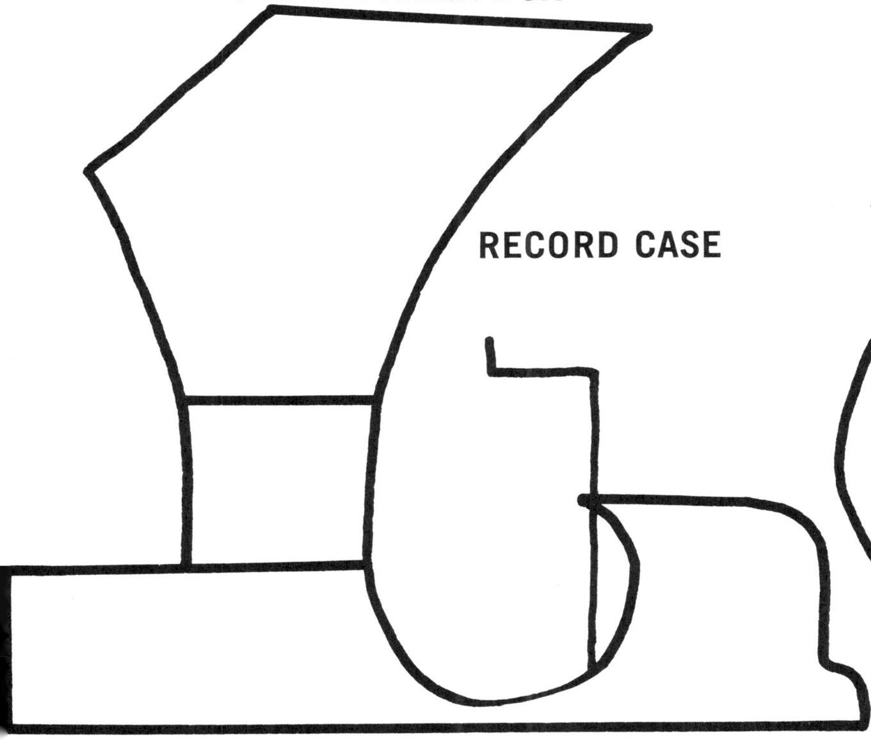

RECORD CASE

(See color plate 13.) ## Picture Frame Box

MATERIALS

flat-hinged metal box	gold embossed paper cut-out
flat paint	ovals and decorative corners
heavy crinkled paper	2 snapshots
dressmaker's carbon paper	rubber cement
gold cord	Sobo and Uhu glue
flocked paper	clear Krylon spray

To paint and cover box

1. Paint the inside and outside edges of a small metal box—ours held little cigars—with flat paint.

Pattern

2. Cover outside with heavy crinkled paper.

3. Trace pattern and transfer to box with white or yellow dressmaker's carbon paper. Use Sobo to glue fine gold cord in place. Dry overnight and spray top, bottom, and sides with clear Krylon.

To line box

4. Cover inside, top, and bottom with flocked paper, cutting the top piece about $\frac{1}{8}$ inch narrower and shorter than the lid so that the box will close tightly.

Photographs and decorations

5. Cut 2 snapshots to fit into gold-embossed paper cut-out ovals and use Uhu to glue in place with additional cut-outs in the corners. Cover snapshots and ovals with a sheet of scrap paper. Press and smooth down frequently until dry.

Makeup Box

(See color plate 16.)

MATERIALS

box	bits of down puff
colored paper	boutique trim
yarn	gold lace, fringe, and braid
brass rings	sequins
rufflings	rhinestones
India ink	rubber cement
plastic toothpicks	Uhu glue

1. Cover or use a colored box.

2. Trace pattern, page 172, or draw free-hand. Note that body, trousers, and feet are all made of figure eights. The head is an oval. The arms are C-shaped on the outside and approximately right-angled on the inside. Be sure to trace around the box for the exact shape before beginning to draw the design.   ***Pattern***

3. Cut out figure from colored paper and cement in place.   ***Figure***

4. Make hair of yarn, earrings of brass rings and rhinestones. Draw eyes and eyebrows with pen and ink. Practice on piece of scrap paper first.   ***Hair and face***

Make veil of ruffling.

5. Make lipstick brush and eyebrow pencils from bits of plastic toothpicks, the ends dipped in ink. Draw eyelash brush with pen and ink. Glue bits of a down puff in place for a powder puff. Make jewelry and decorate costume with boutique trim, gold lace, gold braid, rhinestones, sequins, beads, and gold fringe.

Reprinted from *Seventeen*

Reprinted from *Seventeen*

Curler Caddy

MATERIALS

box
colored paper
gummed reinforcements
yarn
notarial seals

India ink
polka-dot ribbon
rubber cement
Uhu glue

1. Cover box.

2. Trace pattern and cut heads from paper. Make curlers of gummed reinforcements and hair of yarn. Cut features from notarial seals.

3. Draw arrows with India ink.

Box sides   4. Cement wide polka-dot ribbon around sides.

(See color plate 16.) ## Lipstick Box

MATERIALS

bath-powder box
2-ply bristol board
colored paper
2 shades pink tissue paper

moss-green velvet ribbon
rubber cement
Uhu glue
mending tape

Lid to hold lipsticks   1. Use bath-powder box that came with a puff. Put box on bristol board and draw around it. Cut out inside of line so that circle will fit into box.

2. On underside of circle divide it into 6 equal segments and draw around a lipstick on each division line. Cut holes with paper punch to make scalloped effect. Vary size of holes for small and big lipsticks.

3. Glue circle in box to thin ledge where paper once supported powder puff.

To cover and line box   4. Line inside of box and cover outside; cut circles for top and bottom and a wide strip for sides. Cement in place. Glue velvet ribbon around edge of top.

Carnations   5. Stack 4 sheets of tissue paper, 2 light pink, 2 dark. Use a compass to draw 2 concentric circles with a $3\frac{1}{4}$-inch and $1\frac{3}{4}$-inch radii. Cut out with pinking shears. Draw dotted lines to form 24 spokes (see diagram).

Cut slits on dotted lines. Do *not* remove small triangular shapes between petals. Restack circles so that petals are not directly above one another. Pinch center to form a cone, twist, and wrap end with mending tape. Separate petals. Arrange in center of tray and on top of box. Use Uhu to glue in place.

Reprinted from *Seventeen*

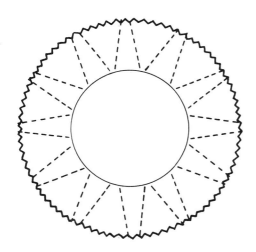

Drawer Box

(See color plate 13.)

MATERIALS

box
plain and decorated paper
heavy cardboard

umbrella tassel
rubber cement
Uhu glue

1. Use a corrugated box which is made of a rectangle sleeve into which another box is fitted. Be sure inside box fits very loosely; when it has been covered with paper it will fit more tightly.

To prepare box

2. Remove inner box; cut off any extra flaps. Cut ¼ inch from upper edge and, if necessary, cement and tape box together to form a drawer.

To make drawer

3. Cut rectangle of heavy cardboard to exact outer measurements of sleeve and glue to front of drawer. Cut and attach second rectangle to back of sleeve.

4. Cover sleeve, line, and cover drawer with decorated papers. Cement in place.

To cover and line box and drawer

5. Punch hole in drawer front and insert strings from umbrella tassel. Tie strings in large knot so that tassel can be used as drawer pull.

Tassel

Reprinted from *Seventeen*

Trinket Box

MATERIALS

egg carton (see photograph)	colored metallic cord
poster paint	gold braid
gold signal dots	colored paper
cardboard	colored tissue paper
masking, Scotch, and	rubber cement
plastic tapes	Uhu glue

1. Select a sturdy, molded egg carton. Cut off flaps from the front of the bottom half.

Interior   2. Paint interior with poster paint. Use it fairly thick and brush in well so that no puddles form. As paint begins to dry, check fit of lid occasionally and press back in shape if it warps. Dry overnight.

3. Glue gold signal dots to top of each post.

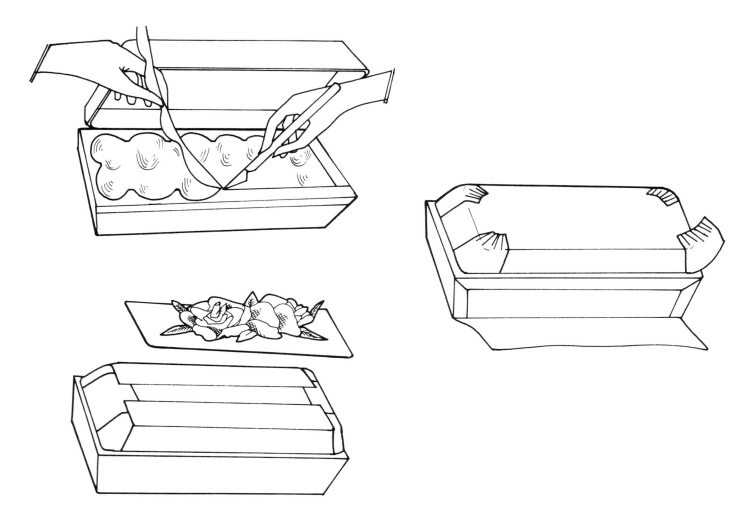

4. Cut strips of cardboard to fit over sides of lower half of box. Tape to bottom with masking tape and to top edge with plastic tape. Trim tape to fit around egg hollows, and add a narrow strip of tape along inside back edge. Trim it to fit around hollows (see diagram). Line edge of hollows with green metallic cord. Cover lower half of box with paper.

Exterior base

5. Give lid 2 coats of rubber cement before covering. Cut 4 strips of paper $1\frac{3}{4}$ inches deep and $2\frac{1}{2}$ inches long. Curve lower edges and fringe top edges as in diagram. Cement these over sides of corner of lid. Overlap fringe on top corners and cement down. Cover areas between corners with strips of paper.

Lid

6. Cut rectangles to fit top and curve corners. Cement paper over it and under its edges. Cement rectangle to top of box. Trim lid's edge with gold braid as in photograph.

7. Cut a strip of yellow tissue paper 20 x $7\frac{1}{4}$ inches. Fold in half lengthwise, then fold it again into eighths and cut as in diagram. You now have 2 scalloped strips.

Roses

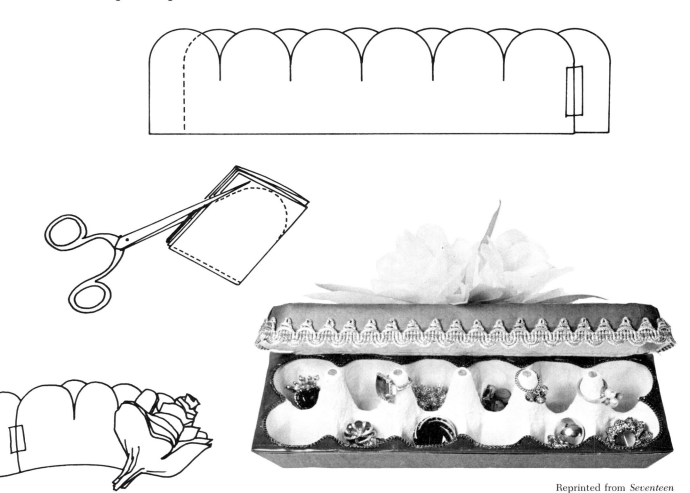

Reprinted from *Seventeen*

Tape them together off center as shown. Begin to roll tightly for center bud; then pinch-pleat or gather the paper as you roll. For fullness, as you make each gather, tape it at the base.

Gently open and curl back petals.

To attach   8. Glue roses in place. Cut leaves of 2 or more shades of green tissue. Crease down center. Glue between roses; allow ends to project.

(See color plate 13.) ## Letter Box

MATERIALS

box	fine gold cord
foil paper	rubber cement
plain and decorated paper	Uhu glue
gold-embossed paper cut-out	plastic tape
letters, keyhole, and key	

To prepare box   1. Use box with hinged lid, such as those in which liquor bottles are sometimes packed. Reinforce hinge inside and outside.

Foil edging   2. Cut strips of foil paper and cement along lower edges, around box over hinge, and along edges of lid. When dry, carefully cut line between lid and bottom. Press foil down along edge.

To cover and line box   3. Line and cover box.

Letters and decorations   4. Decorate with embossed paper, cut-out letters, keyhole, and key. Use Uhu to glue in place. Add fine cord for chain.

Reprinted from *Seventeen*

Record Case

MATERIALS

box	plastic yarn needle
corrugated paper	map tacks
plastic tape	tinsel-covered wire
colored and decorated paper	Uhu glue
plastic 45-RPM adapters	rubber cement

1. Find box big enough to hold records upright, or cut a corrugated box to size. Add doors and hinges.   ***Box and doors***

2. Cover edges of box and doors with plastic tape (see Bangle Box).   ***To cover***
3. Cement paper—cut with scallop or pinking shears as in drawing —in place.

4. Line box and doors. Cement corrugated paper to floor and ceiling, being careful that grooves begin at the same place along the walls so that the records will stand upright.   ***To line***

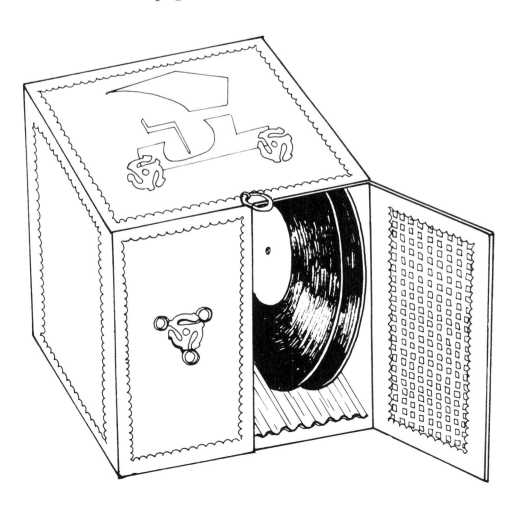

Decorations   5. Trace pattern and cut car from paper. Cement parts in place. Use Uhu to glue 45-RPM adapters for wheels and a bent plastic yarn needle for steering post (heat in hot water to soften, then bend).

Door knob   6. Make knobs of map tacks. Glue in place with Uhu. Snip off points. To lock doors: twist tinsel-covered wire into a small figure eight and slip over 2 top knobs.

Paper-Clip Box for Desk

MATERIALS

box	gold-embossed paper
decorated paper	cut-out letters
felt	rubber cement
lightweight cardboard	Uhu and Sobo glue

1. Use a box for a pen and pencil set. Use cement to cover box with paper. Use Sobo to line with felt.

2. Cut a strip of lightweight cardboard the width of box, and pleat to fit inside.

Divider

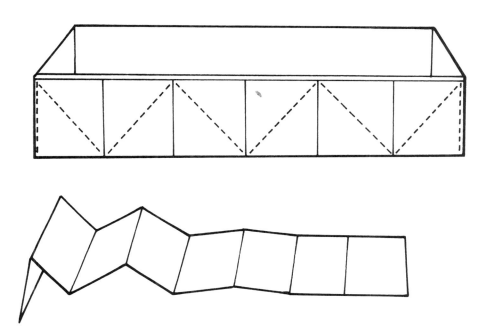

For measurements, draw a line on side of box $\frac{1}{4}$ inch from top. Mark side into 6 equal parts with vertical lines as in diagram. Draw diagonal line. Measure length of diagonal line, then length of vertical line. Six diagonals and 2 verticals will give you the correct length of the cardboard strip.

Measure, mark, score, and fold strip. Cover strip with felt. Use Uhu to glue one vertical flap to one end inside box and the other flap to the other end.

3. Use Uhu to glue gold-embossed cut-out initials to lid.

Decorations

(See color plate 5.) # STONE FIGURES

These can be used as decorative objects or as paper weights.

MATERIALS

smooth stones	gift-wrapping yarn
felt-tipped marking pens	Scotch tape
signal dots	Uhu glue
pipe cleaners	silicone adhesive

To prepare stones

1. Select stones with flat areas that can be glued together.
2. Scrub stones until free of all mud. Allow to dry overnight.
3. Experiment with combinations of stones that suggest figures.

To practice drawing

4. Practice drawing features, hair, etc., on an extra stone. Draw lines in pencil and go over them with marking pens.

To construct figures

5. Join parts of figures together with silicone adhesive on heavy stones; glue on lighter ones. When glue is very tacky, press parts together. Follow directions on tube for silicone adhesive. Brace figure against or between heavy uprights. For stone ears and tails, when glue is fairly steady, hold parts in place with strips of Scotch tape.
Allow to dry overnight.

Features

6. Draw in features with marking pens or make them with signal dots.

Whiskers, tails

7. Make whiskers for small animals, pig's and mouse's tails of pipe cleaners.
Make lion's tail of yarn. Knot 3 pieces together. Leave ends on 1 side of knot for tassel. On other side, cut off 2 strands and leave third for tail. Unravel tassel and hold in vapor over steam from spout of teakettle to fluff.

ALTERNATES

Use flat stones for faces. Draw features, hair, and hat with pencil. Go over lines with marking pens. Use these for paper weights.
Flatten pull tabs with a rolling pin. Use silicone adhesive to attach to back of small faces. When dry, hang on cords or leather thongs. Wear as necklaces.

(See color plate 14.) # EGG SHELL MOSAIC PLAQUE

MATERIALS

black cardboard 9¼ x 13 inches	clear Krylon spray
white egg shells	braid
wax paper	picture hanger
water color paints	Sobo glue
(not poster paints)	

***To collect and
prepare shells***

1. Days or even weeks before you are to begin work, start collecting shells. Use them from soft-boiled as well as raw eggs.

2. Wash shells and remove the membrane from the inside. If soft-boiled, soak in water to loosen membrane. Pieces from the sides of the egg are more useful than those from the ends.

***To apply shells
to panel***

3. Cut wax paper into 2 inch squares.

4. Paint the inside of a piece of shell with glue and lay glue side down on the cardboard.

5. Place wax paper over shell and press down firmly until shell is crushed and all pieces lie flat. Repeat process to cover surface.

6. Where large gaps appear between fragments, cover with a second small piece of shell. Crush flat under wax paper as before.

7. Use tweezers to remove as many overlapping fragments as possible.

8. When entire surface is covered and before glue is completely dry, wipe surface gently with a damp cloth to remove glue from top of shell. Do this slowly and carefully. Do not use too much water or it will seep under fragments and loosen them.

To apply design

9. Trace pattern onto panel, item 9, page 23. Wash away smudges with Ivory soap and water.

10. Paint design. As one part dries, repaint it for more brilliance or for deeper shades. Repaint as often as necessary to obtain the effect you want.

To complete panel

11. When dry, spray with 2 thin coats of Krylon. Follow directions on can carefully. Do *not* apply more than 2 coats.

12. Glue cord around the edges.

13. Attach picture hanger to center of upper back of panel.

LAY ON FOLD

(See color plate 12.)
BURLAP "EMBROIDERY"

Decide in advance if you wish to frame this. Buy the frame and cut the board to fit it. Adapt the design to any change in proportions.

MATERIALS

plywood or pressed wood 12 x 22¼ inches	Christmas tie yarn
burlap: plain or adhesive-backed Con-Tact	curtain-fringe balls
	button
wax-paper	felt
wide masking tape	eyelet screws
dressmaker's carbon paper	picture wire
	Sobo glue

To cover board

1. Cut board and cover with burlap. For Con-Tact burlap, follow directions on the paper backing.

For plain burlap, cover board with thin coat of glue. Lay burlap on it and cover with wax paper before pressing smooth with a cloth.

In either case, miter corners and fold fabric over onto the back. Glue down and hold edges in place with masking tape.

Pattern

2. See item 12, page 24. Enlarge pattern by squares and trace (see page 23) onto burlap. If lines are faint, go over them with a soft pencil.

To attach yarn

3. Run generous line of glue along top of one antler. When glue is tacky, press yarn in place. Repeat on lower half of antler. Continue to apply yarn in this way until entire figure is outlined. Cut bits of yarn and glue in place for spots on back.

Flowers

4. Make flowers from curtain-fringe balls, white petals, and colored centers. Cut leaves from green felt and glue one end of each under a petal. Leave other end loose.

Eye

5. Glue button in place for eye.

To hang

6. Frame or screw eyelets into back and hang with wire.

(See color plate 15.) # COLLAGE

MATERIALS

neckties and their linings
felt: pale turquoise, flesh-colored, and maroon
strips of old sheets
dressmaker's trimmings:
  ruffling
  Venice-lace flowers and borders
  gold fringe and braids
  soutache braid
  dressmaker's frog
  sequined metallic guimpe
  tear-drop pearl edging or costume jewelry

cotton batting and small cotton balls
miniature artificial flowers
doll's wig
colored felt-tipped markers
3-ply bristol board
$\frac{3}{8}$-inch plywood rectangle $20\frac{3}{4}$ x $16\frac{3}{4}$ inches
frame
glass to fit it
screw eyes and picture wire
$\frac{1}{4}$-inch-thick strips wood
fine brad nails
Sobo glue

This can be used as a temporary decoration and hung as an unframed panel. If it is to be hung permanently, it must be framed in a shadow box. Decide in advance how it will be used, for it is much easier to cut a wooden background to fit a frame you already have than it is to find a frame to fit a completed panel.

Unless otherwise noted, always apply the glue to the background and spread it evenly with a piece of cardboard. Use a matchbook cover for a small area and a larger piece of cardboard, about 3 x 5 inches, for the wooden background when covering it with felt.

To prepare neckties

1. Take neckties apart. Be careful to remove the linings and open the seams that join them to the ties. Don't be tempted to cut away the seam. You may need every spare bit. Press ties and linings with a steam iron.

Felt for collage

2. Cut a rectangle of turquoise felt 18 x 15 inches and tack to a work board (you can use the background board for this) with push pins. Draw a rectangle 12 x 15½ inches in the center of the felt as a frame for the collage.

To trace pattern   3. Enlarge patterns (both picture and parts) by squares (see item 12, page 24) onto tracing paper. Trace outline of picture in rectangle by punching holes just *inside* line, so that dots will not show on finished collage, with a sharp soft pencil (page 23). Outline the figure and all the parts of the curtain.

Head, shoulders,   4. Cut out patterns for head, shoulder, and arms after tracing from
and arms   picture onto another piece of tracing paper. Pin to flesh-colored felt and cut out, just *outside* the line so that they will cover the dots on the turquoise felt. Glue in place.

Bodice   5. Glue 2 small cotton balls in place for bust. Cut bodice from narrow end of tie. Turn under a narrow edge on the sides of the bodice and iron flat. Gather either side of the bust. Run a separate gather along top of bodice.

   Glue lower half of bodice in place. On the felt, run a line of glue on either side of the bust and along its top. The bodice will not come up to meet the felt of the shoulders. Put a drop of glue between the cotton balls and press the top in place, shaping it over the bust.

Sleeves   6. Cut sleeve patterns from large end of tie. Gather sleeves around the edges. Fill with thin layer of cotton. Be sure that cotton extends into edges of sleeves. Lay a sleeve over outline on felt to check size before knotting gathering thread. Press sleeve gently into place in glue. Be sure that gathered fabric as well as cotton is glued to felt.

Skirt   7. Cut remains of tie in half, overlap halves, and glue together. If tie is too narrow, use a different tie of similar color and pattern for the skirt. Cut out skirt. Turn under edges along the sides and gather at top. Glue top to waistline. Glue edges of sides down. Leave rest of skirt loose.

Apron   8. Cut apron from 2 layers of lining. Glue Venice-lace trim along bottom and 2 sides. Gather top edge and glue over top edge of skirt. Be sure to place at slight angle as in photograph. Let apron hang loose.

Ruffled collar   9. Run ruffling between fingers to curve. Cut ends at sharp angle as in photograph so that collar projects beyond sleeves. Run line of glue along top edge of ruffling. When glue is tacky, press ruffle in place.

Bouquet   10. Cut out flowers or leaves and petals from a piece of Venice lace to form the circle for the background of bouquet. Arrange a few miniature flower clusters in a dome-shaped bouquet. Twist stems together just below flowers and cut off remaining stems. Push stems through Venice-lace flowers and glue both in place on felt. Fill out bouquet with additional flower clusters. Apply drops of glue to stems and undersides of petals. Carefully slip into bouquet so that other flowers will support them until the glue drys and holds them in place.

Features   11. Practice drawing features on a scrap of felt until you are proficient. First draw them lightly with pencil, then go over the pencil lines

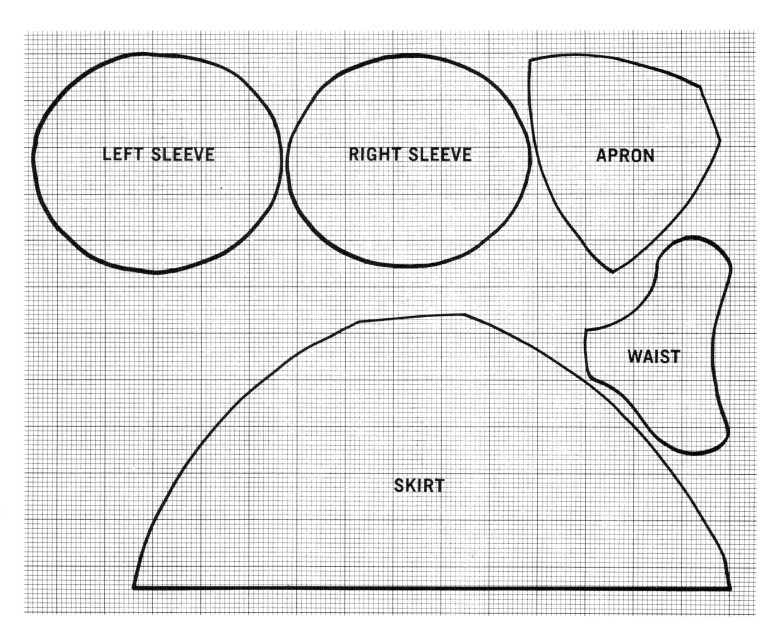

with felt-tipped markers. Make eyes and line of lashes prominent. Use a light hand with mouth, nose, cheeks, and eyebrows.

12. Cut 2 ringlets from wig. Make the coiffure's side puffs and small ringlets from the ends of these. Handle wig gently and place pieces carefully in a generous coating of glue. Divide a 2-inch snippet from the upper section of a ringlet for the hair on the forehead and glue in place. Glue another, larger piece above it for the top knot.

Hair

13. Make earrings from tear-drop pearl edging or costume jewelry. Note that one earring is slightly higher than the other.

Earrings

14. Cut curtain from a second tie. Use an iron to pleat the straight fall on the side of the picture. Glue fall in place along top and edges.

Curtain

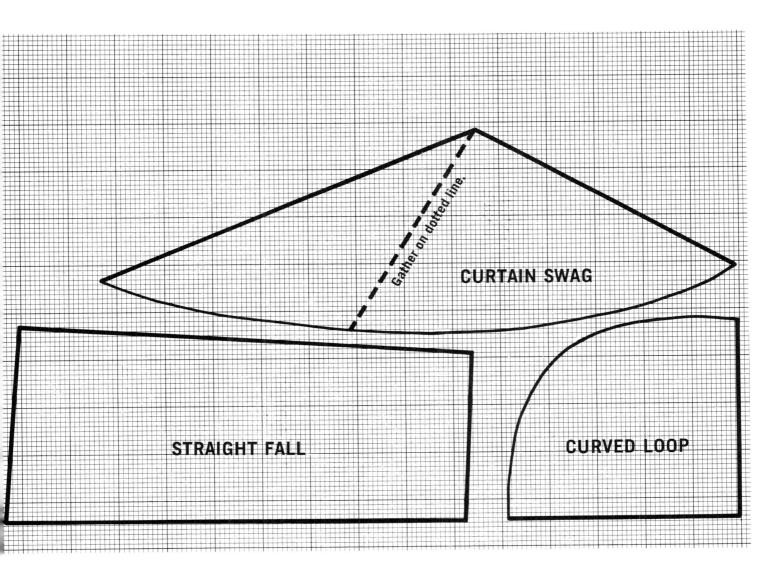

Iron curved pleats into large curved loop and glue in place along edges. Gather the swag along dotted line of pattern. Iron curved and vertical pleats into it and glue in place as in photograph.

Curtain fringe   15. Pull gold fringe between fingers to make fringe slant as though it were hanging down. Then iron, pulling solid edge away from iron to increase slant. Glue along edge of fall. Curve fringe for loop of drapery, slant fringe for upper edge of curve. Repeat process for fringe on swag.

Rosettes   16. Make 2, each from 1 small and 1 large circular Venice-lace flower. Glue in place.

Curtain pull   17. Glue gold cord in place. Attach button-loop half of frog over lower end.

White mat   18. Cut a narrow mat $\frac{1}{2}$ inch wide (inner measurement $11\frac{1}{2}$ x $14\frac{3}{4}$ inches) of 3-ply bristol board. Lay over collage and check that all edges of collage are covered by inside of mat. Don't worry about any that protrude beyond its outer edge. Remove mat and lay to one side.

To cut off edge of collage   19. Use a steel-edged ruler, a triangle, and a single-edged razor blade to be sure that sides of collage are straight and cut at right angles. Trim off excess of felt and fabric so that collage measures 12 x $15\frac{3}{4}$ inches.

Felt and plywood panel   20. If panel is to be mounted in a shadow box, cut the plywood to fit inside the frame's rabbet and cover the front, *not* the edges, with felt.

For an unframed panel, cut rectangle of maroon felt 27 x 23 inches. Center plywood rectangle on felt. Place pins at 4 corners for guides. Cover face of plywood evenly with glue. Lay board, glue side down on felt, using pins as guides. Reverse and smooth felt flat. Turn over again. Glue corners flat on back as in diagram A. Then glue down edges, one at a time, as in B. Hold these overlapping corners in place with push pins until glue and felt are dry.

To attach collage to panel   21. Use a white pencil and draw a rectangle 12 x $15\frac{3}{4}$ inches on the panel. Make border at top and sides all the same width. Lower border should be wider than these. Lay collage in place and hold with push pins along edges. Lift top $\frac{1}{3}$ of collage, spread glue on panel under it, and press top $\frac{1}{3}$ in place. Smooth carefully. Repeat for center and lower $\frac{1}{3}$.

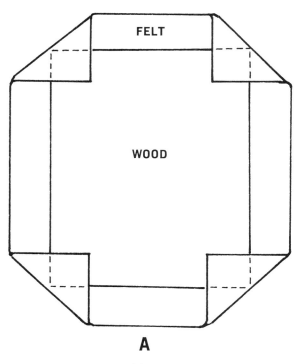

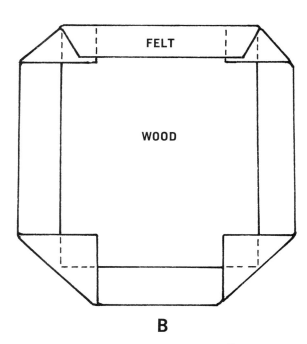

A   **B**

22. Cut ¼-inch-wide strips of maroon felt and glue them around all 4 edges of collage. Spread a thin layer of glue sparingly along edge of collage and strips. Gently press bristol-board mat in place. Be careful that it is centered and that the sides are parallel with the sides of the panel. Repeatedly smooth it with a white cloth to keep it from being buckled when dry.

23. Apply line of glue to *back of gold braid* and lay over outer edge of mat so that it also completely covers felt strips. Pull taut and hold with push pins until dry. Apply glue to *back of soutache braid* and attach to center of gold braid, holding taut with push pins.

24. Attach screw eyes and wire to back of panel for hanging.

25. Lay glass in frame in rabbet. Be sure that glass is spotlessly clean on the inside surface. Measure height of domed bouquet and add ³⁄₁₆ inch to this measurement. Cut the 4 strips of wood this width, 2 long enough to fit inside of rabbet on the long sides of frame and 2 to fit inside at bottom and top. Be sure to deduct the thickness of the wooden strips on the sides from the length of these. Remove strips and drill hole for nails or drive nails in place in each strip. Replace in frame; glue and nail to rabbet.

Border

Screw eyes and wire

Shadow box

Cut strips of maroon felt to cover wood. One at a time, spread the inside surface of each strip of wood with glue, fit felt over it, and smooth. Glue a line of gold braid around the inside, flush with the open edge, to mask the panel. Drill holes for nails around the edge of the panel. Glue and nail panel in place.

To keep dust out of box, cut 2-inch-wide strips of old sheeting, soak in glue, and glue over joints on the outside of shadow box, around the panel, down the side seams, and over the joint where the box joins the frame. Attach screw eyes and wire to the side of the *frame* to hang.

If possible, get a man's help in making the shadow box. If this is impossible and you are overwhelmed by the task, a framer will gladly do it. This will, of course, be more expensive than making it yourself.

ALUMINUM CAN SWANS

MATERIALS

soda and "pop" cans   invisible mending tape
steel washers, 1 inch diameter   signal dots
crayon or china pencil   Uhu glue

You will need a pair of tin shears and a pair of heavy scissors. If possible, beg, borrow or buy a pair of tin shears with compound leverage. These will make the work easier and faster.

Always wear heavy work gloves. Do not allow small children in the room while you are working or until your work has been put away, and the floor and work surfaces have been cleaned. Small slivers of metal may be wiped up with a wet paper towel.

To prepare cans

1. Collect cans with as many different colors, shades, and patterns as possible. Wash thoroughly and allow to dry.

To cut cans apart

2. For soft aluminum cans, cut through rim at the "spout" or opening A in diagram, and cut away the top just along the ridge or shoulder B, diagram 1. Once you have started cutting along B, you can pull up the top at C, diagram 2, with a pair of pliers and carefully pull it off without much cutting. If possible, however, it is wise to enlist a man's help for this. Once the top has been removed, the going is comparatively easy.

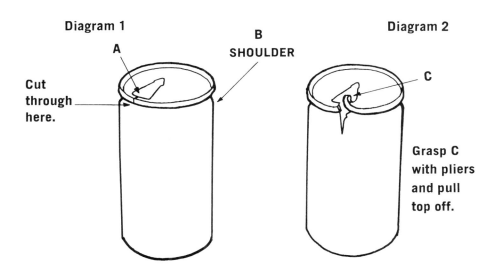

Diagram 1   **B**   Diagram 2
             SHOULDER
        A

Cut
through
here.

Grasp C
with pliers
and pull
top off.

3. Cut down the side of the can to the bottom. Then cut around the bottom to remove it. This can be done with scissors. Flatten out the rectangle of aluminum.

4. On heavier cans, remove the top and bottom with an electric or twist can opener. Cut through rim and along either side of seam. Open can out slightly and cut off top and bottom rims. Flatten out the rectangle of metal.

To trace and cut out swans

5. In either case you are now ready to begin. Fold metal in half crosswise.

6. Trace pattern onto sheet of tracing paper and cut out. Lay pattern on fold as indicated and trace around it with crayon or china pencil.

7. Cut out swan. Fringe wings and tail.

8. Pull sides slightly apart and fold on dotted line. The angle of this line can be varied slightly from bird to bird so that there will be a variety of postures in the flock. If the aluminum should crack along the fold, mend it with tape.

To complete swans

9. Make eyes of signal dots. Bend flaps at right angles to sides and adjust so that the bird will stay upright. Glue washer on flaps to weight the bird and to keep it steady, as shown in drawing.

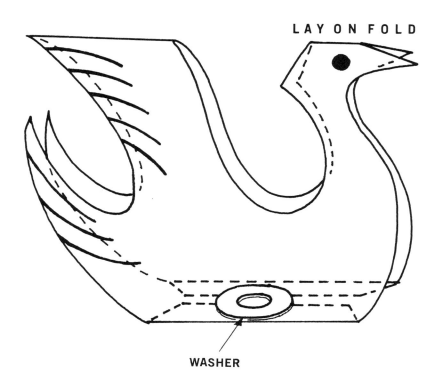

LAY ON FOLD

WASHER

LAY ON FOLD

(See color plate 6.) # MEDIEVAL SPOOL VILLAGE

Junk shops sometimes have large quantities of old spools of thread. The colors are still bright, but the thread has rotted and would break if you tried to sew with it. If you are lucky enough to find such a hoard, you can make this village or part of it for a reasonable sum.

If you do not find them, dowel rods can be substituted for the spools of thread. Sand and paint them with semigloss enamel. Or collect empty spools and paint them.

This project can be made all at one time by a large group, or over a period of months by one or two people. It can, however, more easily be made a piece at a time, adding a new unit each year, for some annual event such as Christmas or a particular family anniversary.

One building and a few trees can be used as a centerpiece year after year. It can do duty also at children's parties, gala adult gatherings at home, or at church, club, or PTA dinners.

MATERIALS

large and small (325 and 125 yard) spools of thread
thin and heavy cardboard
2-ply bristol board
scouring powder cans or salt boxes
base metal (heavy aluminum foil)
felt
pointed and flat-bottom paper cups
1/4-inch dowel rods
1 1/4-inch Styrofoam balls
steel washers
rubber bands
green-enameled florist wire and greening pins (from florist-supply house)
felt-tipped markers

pencil stubs
benzene
tissue paper
colored paper
foil gift-wrapping paper
masking, plastic, Christmas, and gummed-paper tape
gold cord
gold and colored braid
gold dressmaker frogs
straight and glass-headed pins
hatpin
rhinestones
sequins
beads
rubber cement
Uhu and Sobo glue

1. Use Uhu glue to attach steel washers to spools and aluminum foil to cardboard; rubber-cement to join pennants; Sobo glue to join all other materials.

2. Clean washers with benzene before using.

3. Remove loose pieces of spool labels with razor blade; punch label's center into each spool with a dowel. It isn't necessary to clean off labels entirely if glued firmly to spool.

4. Spools are arranged vertically in stacks or horizontally in rows. To make a stack, cut a dowel about 2 inches longer than final height of stack. Glue spools together, and slip stack over dowel. (Dowel ensures a straight stack.) When glue has dried, remove dowel. Rows of stacks are glued side to side.

5. Town hall, houses, major part of cathedral: arrange spools in oblong, and stack to desired height; do not glue yet.

6. Measure inside of oblong and height of gable ends and sides. Cut base, sides, and ends from heavy cardboard. Join with gummed-paper tape (diagram 1). When the roof projects, cut gable end to fit over spools on sides of building (diagram 2). Cover triangular area of frame's gable walls with colored or foil paper matching spools of thread.

7. Cut underbase one spool wider and longer than base, and glue frame to it (diagram 3). This makes a ledge on which to glue spool stacks; underbase won't be visible. Glue spools in stacks; let dry. Gable-end stacks are of different heights, to pyramid.

8. Lay narrow strips of cardboard along underbase edge, to support outer edge of stacks. Glue stacks to underbase, to wall of frame, to each other. Use plenty of glue, but be careful not to spread it where it would show on outside.

9. When all spool walls are glued, slip heavy rubber bands around building. When dry remove rubber bands and cardboard strips.

10. Glue foil-paper circles to tops of gable-end spools if roof doesn't overhang.

11. To make a house with overhanging upper story, cut heavy cardboard rectangle one spool wider and longer than completed lower walls (spools included). Use this for underbase of frame for upper story. Complete frame for upper story; glue its underbase to top of lower walls. Add spool stacks for walls and roof.

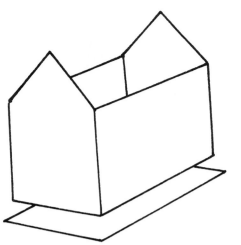

1. FRAME FOR RECTANGULAR BUILDING

3. UNDERBASE FOR SPOOL STACKS

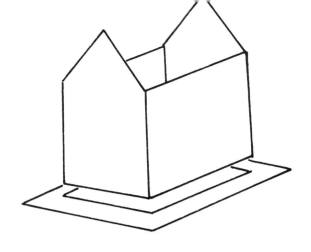

2. GABLE END IF ROOF PROJECTS

4. ROOF FOR RECTANGULAR BUILDING

5. HOUSE WITH OVERHANGING UPPER STORY;
FOUR-STACK TOWER; THIN TOWER;
ROUND TOWER HOUSE

6. SIDE VIEW OF
RECTANGULAR BUILDING

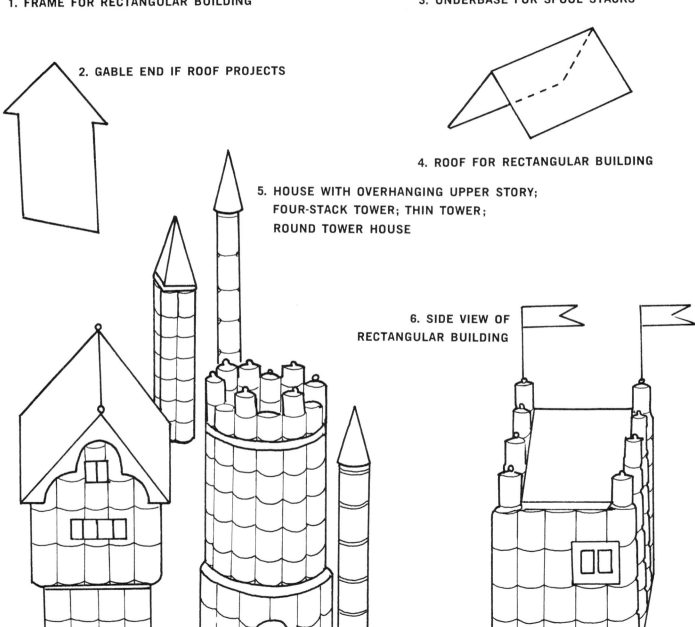

12. Cut 2 cardboard rectangles; join with gummed-paper tape (see diagram 4). Cover outside with felt. Glue roof to gable ends and top of side walls. For round tower house, glue flat, circular roof—covered with foil paper—to top of upper frame. Continue walls above it for parapet. Glue spool to every other spool in top row. Decorate these with beads.

Roofs

13. For each, use as frames 2 empty copper scouring powder cans, ordinary scouring powder cans, or round salt boxes. If there is a gap between the top and bottom of stacked cans, glue scraps of thin cardboard between them. Make underbase as for rectangular building (above). Glue stacks to underbase, frame, and each other.

Large towers

14. Glue half-circles of foil paper to tops of spools. Do not use stacks of spools. Instead, glue a circle of spools, around frame, to underbase. Glue a second circle on first one, placing center of each spool over adjoining edges of spools below it. This gives a checkered effect. Continue the same way until tower is desired height.

Yellow tower

15. At each side, on second-from-top circle, glue a turret made of a single stack of spools. Hold with rubber bands; pour glue, in small quantities, between tower and turrets until space is filled. Do not fill with glue all at once; it might spill down sides.

16. Make 4 stacks, 8 spools high, of different colored small spools. For roof, fold a pointed paper cup in half and then in quarters; trim edge straight. Cover with felt; glue on; decorate with gold braid.

4-Stack tower

17. These are single stacks. So thin towers won't tip over, weight them with washers—4 below and 3 on top of bottom spool. Glue washers to each other and to spool with Uhu glue.

Turrets and thin towers

18. Make larger cones from semicircles of bristol board. Hold cone together with masking tape and staples. Make the smaller roofs from pointed paper cups. Cover with felt. Stuff with glue-dabbed tissue paper.

Tower and turret roofs

19. Cut from colored paper; glue in place. Decorate building with braid, rhinestones, dressmaker frogs, glass-headed pins, beads. For town hall, attach gold frogs to top of gable spools with greening pins and glue.

Doors and windows

20. See diagram, page 151. Fold colored paper. Run glue in fold; lay green-enameled florist wire in it, for flagpole. Rubber-cement paper to-

Pennants

gether. Trim to desired shape; decorate with sequins, colored paper, plastic and Christmas tapes. Glue bead to top of pole. Puncture point of conical roof with heavy needle. Insert flagpole through a bead and then into roof point. Glue.

Cathedral tower

21. Cardboard frame is not necessary. Use 9 stacks of spools, 8 on outside and the ninth in the center for rigidity.

Steeple

22. Cover narrow bristol-board cone and flat-bottom paper cup with felt. Glue gold braid around edge of cup. Glue cone to inverted cup; glue to tower. Insert gold-headed hatpin in steeple point.

Frame

23. See directions for making rectangular buildings. Cut 2 cardboard strips to fit on each side of tower at front of cathedral, and cut 2 gable ends, one for back and one to be glued to back of tower (diagram 7). Cut roof to fit around tower (diagram 8).

Stained-glass windows

24. Spot colors at random, with felt-tipped markers on aluminum foil. Draw around colored areas with black marker. Cut out; mount on thin cardboard $3/16$-inch larger than window all around. Cover this edge with braid. Glue windows in place.

City-gate archway

25. Glue 2 spools to each other and to cardboard strip. Reverse; glue in center of strip 4 spools long. Make 2 4-spool stacks; glue to ends of strip. When dry, reverse; cover top with foil paper, and edge with braid. Cut bristol-board strip one spool wide. Cover with foil paper. Curve into arch, and glue inside gateway opening. Outline arch with braid; decorate area above it with frogs.

City-gate towers

26. Use scouring powder cans for frames. For lower part, use stacks of 8 small spools; for upper, stacks of 2 large spools. There will be a gap between 2 lower stacks of each tower. Fit archway into gaps; glue. Fill in gaps above archway with strips of gold cord.

Town walls

27. The spool town may be surrounded by straight or curved walls. Cut heavy cardboard strips the width of large spool. (For curved walls, it is easier to glue together 2 strips of thin cardboard.) Glue stacks of spools to strip and to each other. Make wall any length desired. When dry, reverse wall; cover top with foil paper; decorate edge with braid.

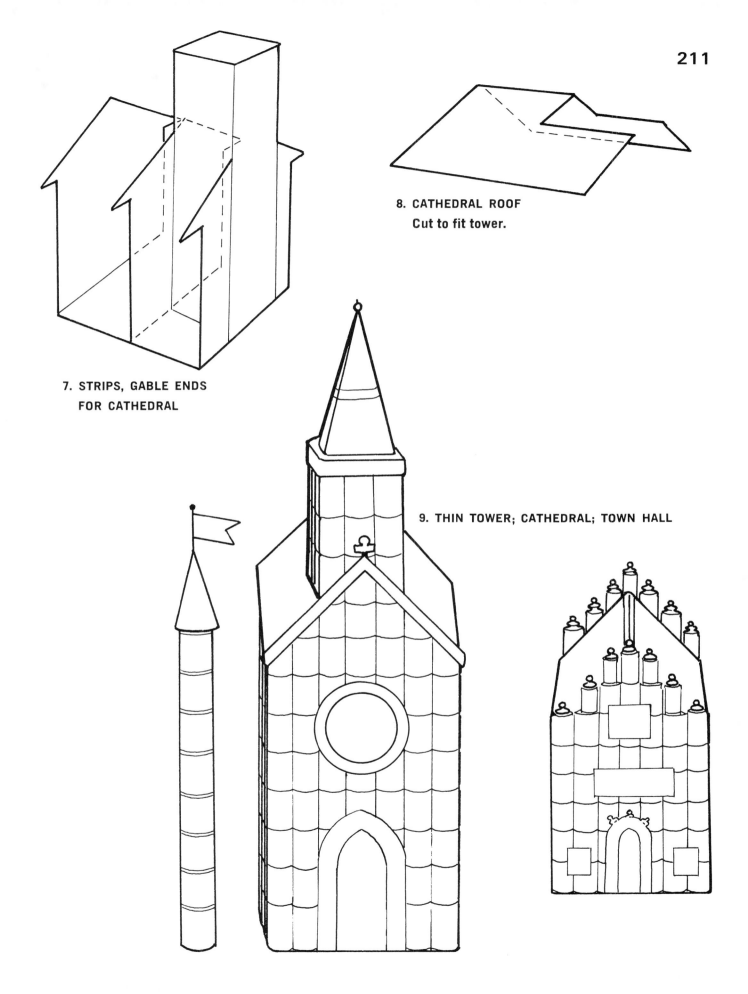

7. STRIPS, GABLE ENDS FOR CATHEDRAL

8. CATHEDRAL ROOF
Cut to fit tower.

9. THIN TOWER; CATHEDRAL; TOWN HALL

10. CITY GATE; WALL WITH ROOF

11. For TREE: cut thread on spool; open out; divide in half; tie each.

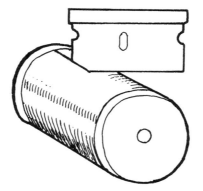

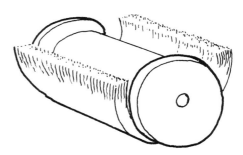

28. Glue large spools to cardboard strip. Reverse; glue 2 rows of small spools to strip. On these, glue small spool to center and one at each end. Make roof; attach to top spools and edge of upper walls. Decorate roof edges with braid wide enough to hide empty space.

Town wall with roof and overhang

29. For each tree, use 6 spools, large or small, of one color or related shades. Fold 1 yard of thread double, then double again, making 4 strands. Twist several times. Set aside.

Tree foliage

30. Follow diagram 11: cut thread on spool with one-edged razor blade. Open cut thread. Divide into 2 bundles. Turn over one; lay on twisted thread. Tie twisted thread by interlocking ends once and then a second time before pulling tight. Repeat to make knot. Shake and fluff thread into pompom.

31. Run a straight pin through twisted thread into bundle and out through knot. Cut off excess twisted thread. Impale a Styrofoam ball on a sharpened pencil stub (black out any color and lettering on stub with felt-tipped marker). Put large drop of glue on ball; stick pin through it, and press pompom firmly against ball. Make 11 more pompoms. Attach to ball.

32. For trees with foliage made from small spools, glue 2 washers to end of small spool (bottom of stand) and 1 washer to other end. For trees with foliage made from large spools, use 5 washers—3 on bottom, 2 on top.

Tree stands

33. Glue circle of gold foil paper on top washer. Cover all washer sides with gold braid. Punch hole through foil paper; insert tree trunk; glue.

34. When tree has dried 24 hours or longer, hold foliage in vapor over steam from teakettle. Shake gently, and fluff with point of scissors. Hang large trees upside down to dry.

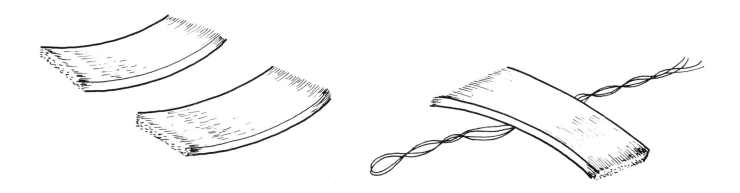

CAT'S ORIENTAL PLAYHOUSE

This makes a decorative place for a cat to hide. It has interior openings from box to box for the animal to go from one room to another, grilles for it to look out, windows to poke its head from, and even a small bell to bat with its paw.

Follow photograph as a guide to the directions.

MATERIALS

corrugated boxes of various
   sizes and shapes
corrugated board
gift-wrapping paper
gift-wrapping ribbon
gift-wrapping cord
notarial seals

small brass bell
plastic lace doilies
dressmaker's braid
bead
rubber cement
Sobo glue

Arrangement   1. Arrange boxes in an interesting complex of forms. Mark carefully where boxes overlap.

Doors and windows   2. Use a sharp knife to cut out central door, a little larger than you will want the final opening. Cut out windows.

Then cut interior openings between boxes. On either side of center box cut a door into the adjoining room. Cut a hole in the ceiling of each of these into the room above. From these make holes into the center box. Cut a hole in its ceiling into the topmost box.

To cover   3. Cement paper over the boxes except for the interior openings. Miter paper over windows, fold paper under, cement, and tape in place. As you complete each box, mark again on the paper where it overlaps adjoining boxes. Be sure that interior holes remain aligned.

Roof   4. Cement rectangles of contrasting paper to the roof and glue ribbons around the edge of boxes.

Doorway   5. Fold rectangles of paper in half and then cut out with pinking shears two Moorish doorways: one large and one small. Make a third,

← **FOLD**

**Fold paper in half.
Draw or cut
doorway freehand.**

smallest cut out for false door to go on top of second cut-out. Cement them together and then to right-hand box. Make rectangular false door for center box on second level. Cement in place.

Trace around inside of largest cut-out onto rectangle of corrugated board for main doorway. Contrast doorway and cover board with paper,

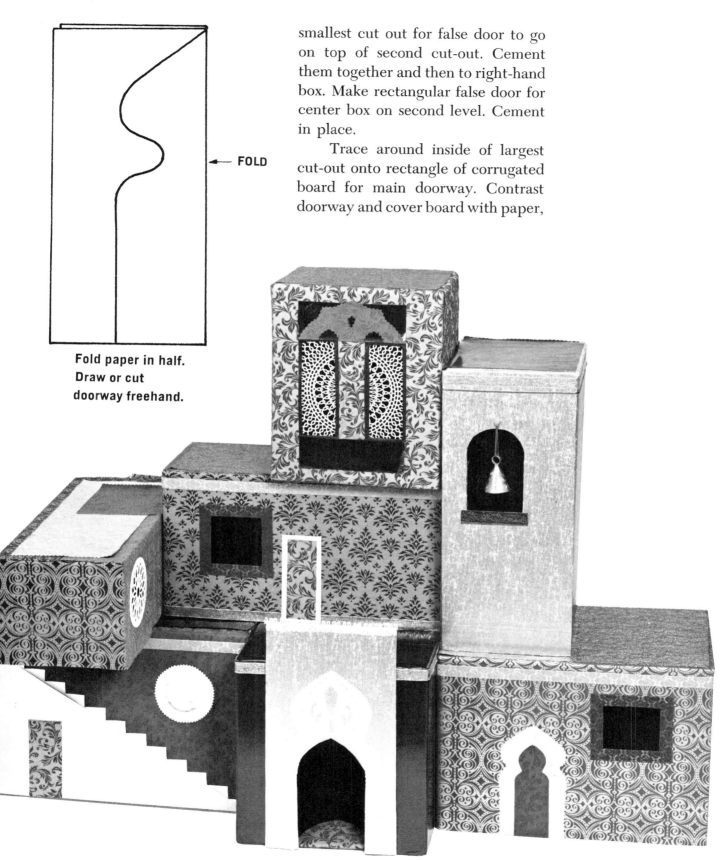

cemented in place. Miter and cement the paper over the opening to the underside of the box. Decorate door frame with lacy cut-outs and paper punch holes, cementing it in place (see item 21, page 28, items 19–20, page 27).

Windows   6. Trim center window frame with cut-out and strips of contrasting paper. Glue a plastic doily securely in place behind it. Glue a second doily securely over window in left-hand box of second level. Use notarial seals to make false window on box below it. Trim remaining windows with ribbon.

Stairs   7. On box with stairs, measure length of diagonal. Cut a strip of paper this length, divide into equal parts, and mark with points. Between these points draw right-angle triangles for steps. Cut out and cement to box. Cut large triangle of a contrasting color to fit below it and cement in place.

Bell   8. Glue and tape a 3-inch square of cardboard on the inside of the box above arched window. Punch a hole through it and box $3/4$ inch above window. Hang bell on metallic cord. Run cord through hole and knot. Glue bead over hole on front of box.

To assemble   9. Glue boxes together along overlap marks. Be sure that interior openings are aligned. Allow to dry 24 hours before permitting cat to enter.

FELT WALL HANGING

(See color plate 2.)

MATERIALS

felt
dressmaker's findings:
    middy braid
    cotton loop braid
    woven band
    cotton cord frog
    small Venice-lace flowers
    rickrack

sequins
tiny bead
tracing paper
colored pencil
toothpicks
wooden lath, 38 inches long
Sobo glue

1. Cut rectangle of felt 36 x 19½ inches. Be sure corners are square. Fold under 2 inches along top edge and iron flat.
To cut background

2. Trace design pages 218–19 and enlarge by squares (see item 2, page 24) on tracing paper.
To enlarge patterns

3. Trace onto background (see page 23). Draw line 1/16 inch *inside* outline so that it will not show when pieces are glued down.
To trace design on background

Reprinted from *Better Homes and Gardens Christmas Ideas*

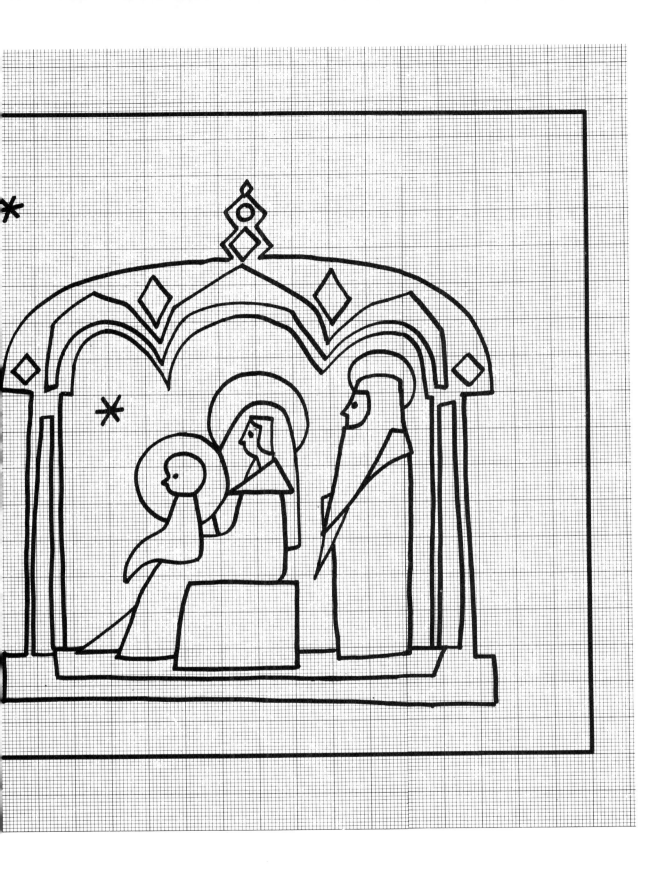

***To trace and
cut-out parts***

4. Trace individual shapes in *reverse* (turn the patterns over before tracing) on the *back* of felt, so that lines will not show on right side. Use light pencil on dark pieces and dark pencil on light pieces. Cut out shapes a fraction of an inch larger than outline.

***To check parts
and arrangement***

5. Arrange pieces in place on background with trimmings to check size, positions, colors, etc. Parts may overlap or interlock, but small parts are best glued on top of large ones.

Interlock rickrack, glue ends together, and trim ends for Ethiopian king's robe. With needle and thread, gather lower points of a short piece of rickrack to make knob on hat of Oriental king. Stars are made of small Venice-lace flowers. Eyes are sequins.

To attach

6. Glue parts in place, using a thin layer of glue and spreading it with a toothpick. If drop of glue falls on felt, allow it to dry untouched and then pick it off. Dry hanging overnight. Using pressing cloth, iron on a padded surface.

To hang

7. Lay hanging face down on flat surface. Lift fold at top of felt and lay lath just below crease. Run a generous line of glue along under edge of felt. Lay flap of felt over lath and press edge against back of hanging. Allow to dry thoroughly. Support each end of lath with tack or hook in wall; or hang from cord, tied to each end of lath.

MIRROR IN SHELL-DECORATED FRAME

(See color plate 11.)

MATERIALS

Polaroid film pack
small, round pull tab from soft-
    drink can
purse mirror 2½ x 3½ inches
tiny shells, bits of coral,
    shark scales

small pearl beads
cotton ball
dark blue-gray spray paint
cardboard
Uhu glue

1. Use rolling pin to flatten pull tab.   *Pull tab*

2. Separate pack into 3 parts. Spray parts 1 and 2 and the pull tab   *To paint frame*
with paint. It is not necessary to paint the inside of part 1, but be sure
all edges of both parts are painted. Allow to dry.

3. Using tweezers, arrange shells, coral, and shark scales on frame.   *Shells*
When arrangement is satisfactory, glue each piece in place.

4. Glue small pearl beads in place.   *Pearls*

5. Lay part 1 over part 3. Be sure that part 3 is resting on its flanges   *Mirror*
so that its surface is flush with opening in part 1.

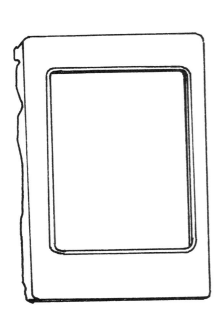

1

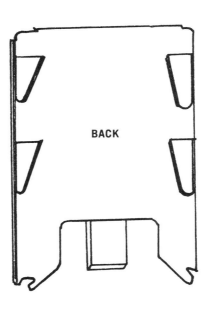

BACK

2

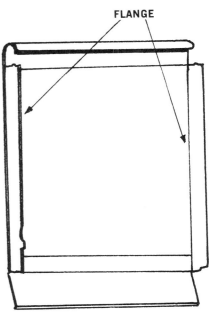

FLANGE

3

6. Lay mirror in place on part 3; with a white pencil mark where each corner rests.

7. Remove part 1. Using white corner marks as guides, glue mirror in place on part 3.

To assemble

8. Replace part 1 over part 3. Press down elongated triangles of part 2 and slip part 2 in place.

Pull tab

9. Glue pull tab to upper center of back for hanging.

Easel

10. Glue a triangular easel (see item 25, page 29) to lower center of back so that frame can also stand upright on a flat surface.

ALTERNATE

Glue photograph on mat and substitute for mirror on part 3.

SHELL BOUQUET IN SHADOW BOX

(See color plate 10.)

MATERIALS

Polaroid film pack
small, round pull tab from soft-
    drink can
gilt spray paint
black plastic tape
shells, shark scales, and bits
    of coral

tiny pearl beads
heavy turquoise paper
gauge 21, green-enameled florist
    wire
cotton ball
cardboard
Uhu glue

1. Roll pull tab flat with rolling pin. ***Pull tab***

2. Separate pack into 3 parts (see diagrams, page 221). Spray pull tab and parts 1 and 2 with gilt paint. ***To prepare pack***
3. Press long, triangular tabs on part 2 flush with back; cover them on the outside with tape.
4. Cut off flanges of part 3 with metal shears.

5. Cut piece of turquoise paper to fit over part 3 and glue it to it. Lay part 1 over part 3 and with a fine pencil draw a very light outline of the opening on the paper. Remove part 1. ***Background***

6. Curl wire by drawing a long piece between thumb and forefinger. Do not try to curl a little at a time or you will get a bumpy curve. Cut small pieces of wire for the 3 long stems; glue in place. ***Stems***

7. Cut out circles $\frac{1}{4}$ to $\frac{3}{16}$-inch diameter from turquoise paper. Using tweezers, arrange bivalve shells in a circle on one of them to form a flower. Glue shells to paper. When these are dry, glue a circle of smaller shells in the center. Allow to dry and glue a tiny shell or bead in the center of these. Repeat for additional flowers. ***Compound flowers***

8. Arrange bouquet on part 3; keep design well within pencil lines. Use a scallop shell for vase. Glue a bit of cotton inside it. This will attach it more securely, with glue on both the shell rim and the cotton, and also ***To arrange bouquet***

raise it enough along the top edge to give the illusion that the bouquet comes out of it.

To glue bouquet 9. Glue compound flowers in place. Glue tiny snails (gastropods) along stems to suggest flowers. Finally, add coral, stray shells, and shark scales to fill out bouquet.

To assemble frame 10. Place frame, part 1, over bouquet, part 2. Spread glue over part 3 and slip in place over back edge of frame. Carefully press part 2 into the glue on part 3. Allow to dry.

Pull tab 11. Glue pull tab to upper center of back for hanging.

Easel 12. Glue and tape a triangular cardboard easel (see item 25, page 29) to lower back so that frame can also stand upright on a flat surface.

SPATTER PICTURE

Decide in advance if you wish to frame this. Buy the frame and cut the board to fit it. This will be less expensive than having a frame made for the finished picture.

MATERIALS

white cardboard (ours is
   20 x 30 inches)
leaves, ferns, and grasses
India ink
toothbrush
paring knife

straight pins
masking tape
2 picture hangers
tracing paper
newspaper

Background

1. Measure a border 2½ inches wide around both sides and top of cardboard and 3½ inches deep at bottom. Draw lines with a fine light pencil.
2. Cover the border with tracing paper, held along the pencil lines with tape. Be careful that tape lies exactly on line and is pressed flat.
3. Spread newspaper over work area and lay board in place.

To arrange greens on board

4. Arrange ferns, grasses, and leaves for picture. Select those you want to predominate—they will be the whitest. Pin these in place and remove the others. Do not try to pin greens absolutely flat. Shading will occur where the edges are slightly raised. This adds the illusion of depth.

To spatter

5. Pour a tablespoon or more of ink into a cup's saucer. Dip the tip of the toothbrush bristles in it. Be careful not to overload bristles.

It is wise to wear rubber gloves and an apron when spattering. Draw the paring knife across the bristles to make a fine spray to spatter the paper.

6. When you have confidence in controlling the spray, begin to spatter around and over the greens. Keep spray fine and cover the area around the greens with a light gray. Proceed to cover the complete background with it. Allow to dry *thoroughly*.

7. Pin another layer of greens over the first and spray again. Dry thoroughly and repeat until the picture is complete. Note that the grays are modulated over the surface of the finished picture.

8. Be absolutely sure that everything is dry before lifting off greens and pins. Carefully remove masking tape and tracing paper.

To hang   9. Picture can be framed under glass or can be hung temporarily from 2 picture hangers glued to either side of the upper back.

ALTERNATES

Colored inks in a variety of combinations can be used in the same picture.

Liquid textile dyes can be used on fabrics. These can be dry-cleaned and can be used on dress and light upholstery fabrics.

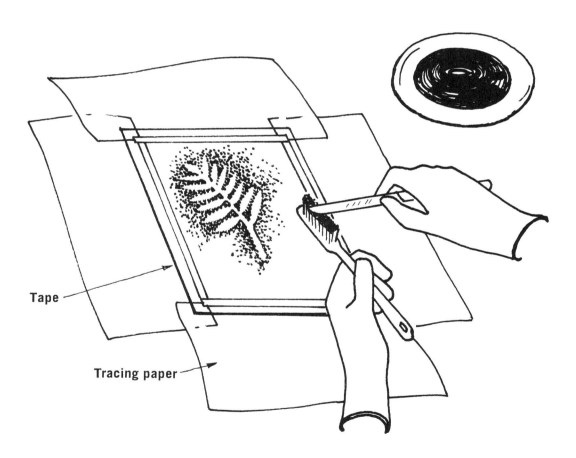

Tape

Tracing paper

(See color plate 11.) # NECKLACE I

MATERIALS

opaque plastic electric-typewriter ribbon spools
soutache braid
beads

brass upholstery nails
thread
Uhu glue

To attach spools

1. Knot a spool in the center of a 3-yard length of soutache braid by following diagrams 1–7. When knot is complete, sew it closed across the back before proceeding to next spool.

2. Continue to attach spools as indicated above. Balance them in groups of 1 or 2 on either side of center bead. Do not try to make the lengths between groups on either side match exactly.

To join ends

3. Attach 13 spools. Try on necklace and adjust length. Cut off excess braid, making one end about 2 inches longer than other. Overlap remaining ends ½ inch and sew securely together on both sides for entire length of overlap.

To attach last spool

4. Attach spool as in diagrams 8–13. Adjust braid so that the overlap is hidden on the back of the spool and pull knot tight. Sew sides of knot securely together across the back.

Beads

5. Use 3 large faceted beads for the 3 center spools. Glue an upholstery nail in the hole of each bead and each bead in the center of a spool.

6. Use 6 smaller, lighter (plastic or hollow) beads in next 3 pairs of spools. Glue in place on the braid.

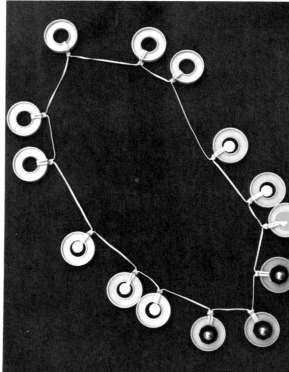

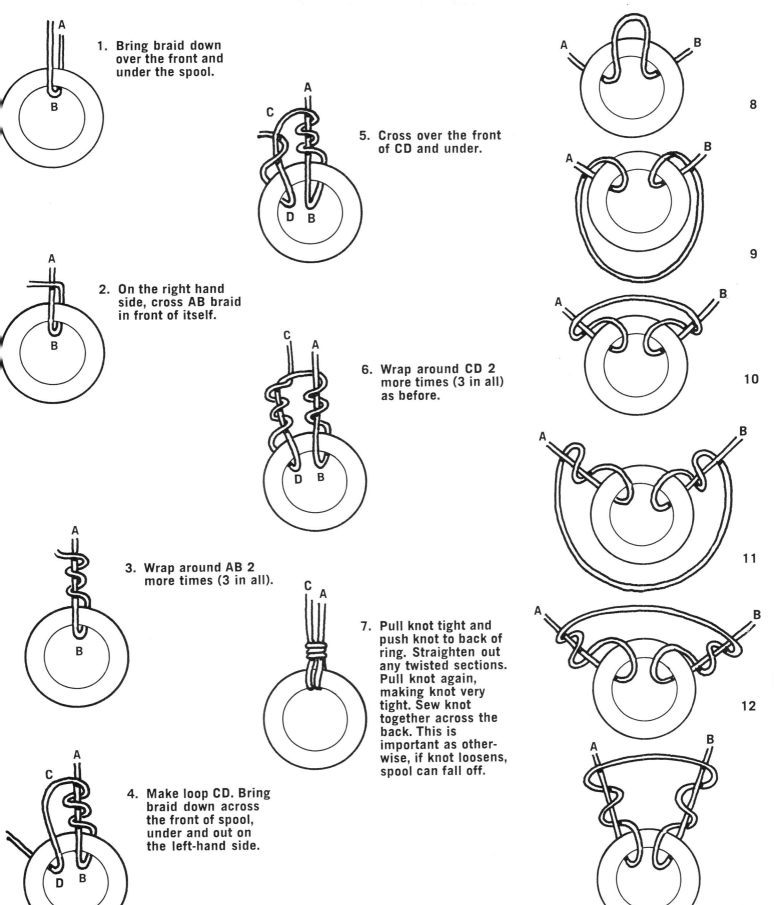

1. Bring braid down over the front and under the spool.

2. On the right hand side, cross AB braid in front of itself.

3. Wrap around AB 2 more times (3 in all).

4. Make loop CD. Bring braid down across the front of spool, under and out on the left-hand side.

5. Cross over the front of CD and under.

6. Wrap around CD 2 more times (3 in all) as before.

7. Pull knot tight and push knot to back of ring. Straighten out any twisted sections. Pull knot again, making knot very tight. Sew knot together across the back. This is important as otherwise, if knot loosens, spool can fall off.

8

9

10

11

12

13

NECKLACE II

MATERIALS

metallic gift-wrapping cord
gift-wrapping yarn
small brass bell
brass polish

lacquer spray
various colored button
  and carpet thread
Uhu glue

To prepare bell   1. Polish bell and spray with lacquer.

To braid   2. Cut 80-inch lengths of red, gold, and green cord. Pin ends together with 2 or more push pins to work table. Braid cords, A. When braid is 12 inches long, slip 2 cords through ring at top of bell and continue to braid until finished, B.

Sew 3 cords together securely at both ends of braid, C. Knot matching cords from the 2 ends together. Flatten knots against cord; point loose ends toward bell. Sew knots tightly to braid and cut off loose ends, E.

Cord tassel   3. Cut 15-inch lengths of cord, 2 of each color. Slip them through an opening in braid above knots. Pull the 6 lengths over the knots and flatten against braid. Be sure that ends are even. Pull string from a 12-inch length of red cord. Iron cord flat, cover one side with glue, and wrap around the braid and the 12-inch lengths. Glue end flat, F.

Tassels   4. Make tassel by wrapping yellow, orange, and red yarn each around a card 3¾ inches wide (see item 27, page 29). Wind the orange a few times more than the other 2 for a heavier center tassel. At one end of card tie yarn tightly together with a 36-inch length of matching thread. Cut yarn along opposite side of card.

Remove string from 9-inch length of cord of related color (gold for yellow, red for orange, silver for blue), iron flat, and cover one side with glue. Wrap cord tightly around yarn to form tassel.

Braid   5. Cut one 20-foot, one 10-foot length each of red, gold, and green cord. Securely sew one end of each 10-foot length to the midpoint of the same color 20-foot length and fold the 20-foot length in half to make three

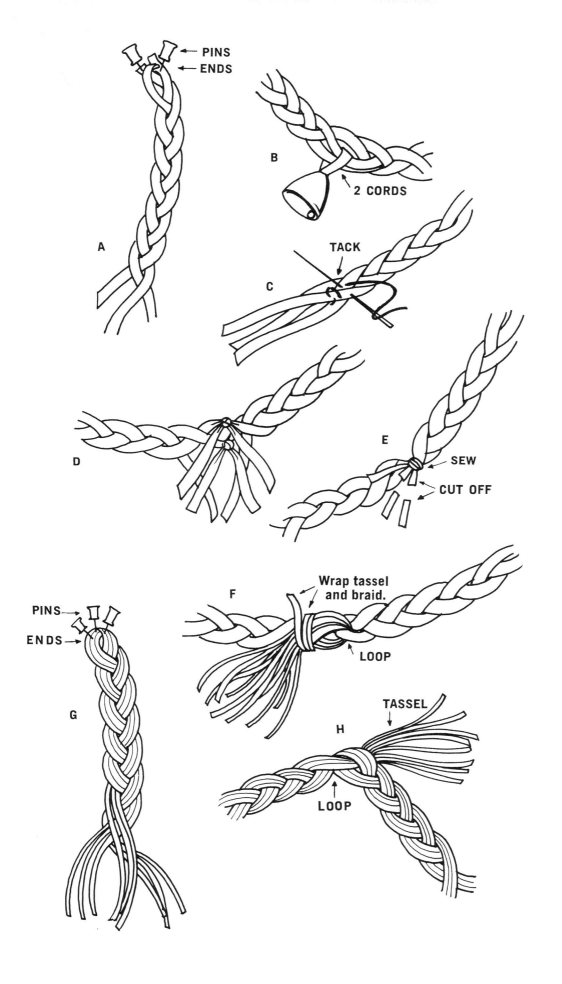

PINS

ENDS

A

B

2 CORDS

TACK

C

D

E

SEW

CUT OFF

F

Wrap tassel
and braid.

LOOP

G

PINS

ENDS

H

TASSEL

LOOP

10-foot strands. Treating each color group as a strand, fasten them with push pins to a work table and braid, G. When 2 inches from end, sew all the braids together. Remove string from cord from 1 inch of the ends. Pull this tassel through the loop where you started braiding and sew loop and tassel securely together, H.

To attach tassel   6. Arrange tassels as in photograph, heavier orange tassel in center, and sew to braid.

NECKLACE III

(See color plate 11.)

This can be worn high around the throat, as a collar, or lower, as a pectoral on the upper chest. As fashions change, so can the shape of the necklace. See diagram 2 for suggested variations.

MATERIALS

heavy felt
soutache braid
thread
costume jewelry, whole or parts
beads

rhinestones
pearls, singly or in fine
 strands
Sobo glue

1. Cut out 2 pieces of felt (pattern, page 235); sew 14-inch length of braid securely to either end of one piece (see diagram 1).

2. Spread generous layer of glue over entire surface and spread second piece on top of it.

Felt background

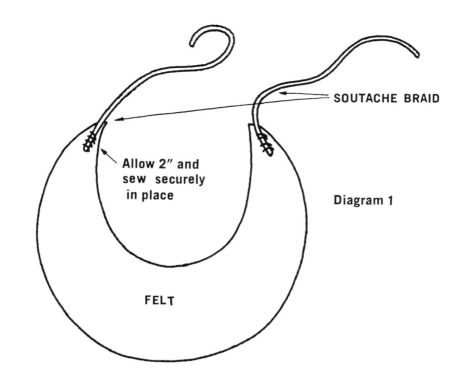

SOUTACHE BRAID

Allow 2" and
sew securely
in place

Diagram 1

FELT

SUGGESTED VARIATIONS

Diagram 2

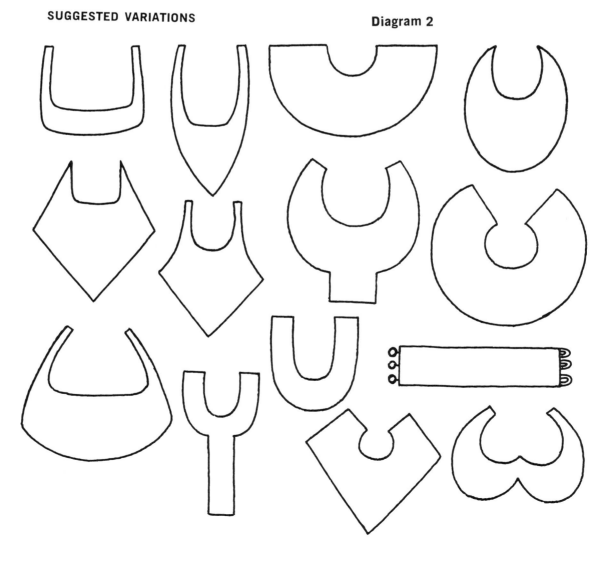

3. While glue dries, arrange decorations. If making a large unit, such as the center of this one, glue parts on a separate piece of felt. Cut out felt around the edge of the unit. It will be easier to handle this way than in small pieces and can be glued directly on background. *Decorations*

4. When decorations have been arranged, start in the center and glue the large pieces in place. Then attach outlines such as pearl strands. Last, fill in with the small individual beads, rhinestones, and spangles.

5. Run line of glue around felt edge, and when glue is tacky, press strands of small pearls in place. Note that the inner pearl edging stops about an inch from the back points. This makes the fastening at the back less cumbersome. Sew through both layers of felt and through braid at either end and sew around group of jewelry in center. *Pearl edging*

6. Glue the ends of the braid into hollow gold beads. *Braid ends*

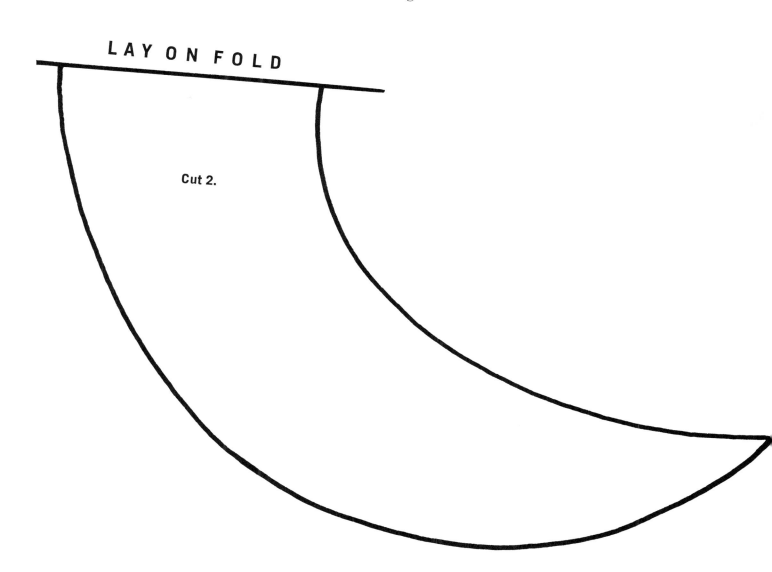

LAY ON FOLD

Cut 2.

PENDANT

MATERIALS

heavy cardboard 3¼ x 3⅛ inches

silver gift-wrapping metallic cord

silver gift-wrapping foil paper

silver beads

thread

rubber cement

Uhu glue

To cover

1. Cement paper over front of cardboard, miter corners, and fold over 1 inch on back. Cement to back. Cut 3 x 3-inch square of foil and cement on back.

With an ice pick, punch holes in the upper corners, ¼ inch from sides and top edges.

Trace pattern from page 237. Trace onto pendant with blunt pencil.

To apply cord

2. Cut strips of cord, cover one side with glue, and wrap cord tightly into spirals. Leave from 1 to 10 inches loose at end. On some strips, make a spiral at both ends.

Cover back of spiral with glue. Use a toothpick to cover a short bit of the same edge of the loose cord with glue. Lay spiral in place and curl loose cord along the design. Hold in place until glue is dry. Apply glue to more cord and press in place. Continue until that section of design is complete and then repeat process on another section.

To insert cord between spiral and adjacent cord, cut cord at angle and glue so that pointed end is on top (see diagram, page 238).

Feel free to vary the design as you work. It would be tedious and pointless to repeat the pattern exactly.

Glue a strip of cord around pendant, beginning and ending on lower edge. Cut strings from end (see diagram), flatten cord, and glue together in overlap for an even finish.

To incise background

3. Use a strong pointed toothpick to incise fine circular lines on background.

To make cones

4. Cement 2 rectangles of foil paper back to back and cut out 5 circles of 1-inch diameter. Slash each circle to center and roll into cone. Cement

Courtesy of NORCROSS DESIGN STUDIOS

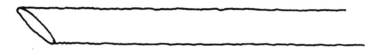

1. To insert cord between coil and adjacent cord, cut cord
   at angle and glue so that the pointed end is on top.

2. Where ends of cord are exposed, push metallic tube back
   to expose string filling.

3. Cut off 1″ of string and pull tube back in place. For
   overlap, glue flattened ends on top of one another.

down ends, but allow base to be slightly uneven. Later, cone will open
and coil will hang loose.

To attach cones   5. Thread needle, make heavy knot in thread, and run needle and
thread through tip of cone from the underside. Push needle at angle into
bottom edge of pendant and out through the back. Allow $\frac{3}{8}$-inch length
of thread below pendant and glue 1-inch length to pendant back.

Beads   6. Glue 3 sizes of beads to center of spirals, varying the size with
the size of the spirals.

Cord for neck   7. Run a long length of cord through holes at top of pendant, so that
ends of cord come out on the back. Make a knot 1 inch from one end.
Try on in front of mirror to adjust length of cord. Make second knot at
back of pendant. Cut off 1 inch from knot. Glue knots to back.

INDEX

INDEX

Study index for suggestions and additional uses for projects, such as listings for centerpieces and favors. Look up specific scrap materials for projects using them. Use lists, such as animals, birds, and figures, for ideas from which to improvise. If you are unsure of drawing or making a figure, the entries under pictures may give you courage to simplify the shape you wish to produce. Figures listed under ornaments should be hung with nylon line or thread for tree decorations.

Color plate references and photographs will be found with the text of each project.